In the Wake of the Golden Galleons

ABOUT THE AUTHORS

ROY VOLKER is the president of two firms dealing in treasure hunting. Search Electronics is the Midwest distributor for White's treasure-hunting equipment. It also deals in a wide range of treasure-hunting services. At the head of Golden Royal Enterprises, he is in charge of a sea-going treasure-hunting firm, working out of Nassau, The Bahamas. He is a former big game hunter, prospector and professional prize fighter.

DICK RICHMOND is an editor and columnist for the St. Louis Post-Dispatch. Before joining the Post-Dispatch, he was a photographer with United Press International. As a writer and as a photographer, he has material published in almost every major publication in the United States. For the last several years Richmond has shared all of Volker's treasure-hunting adventures.

In the Wake of the Golden Galleons

Roy Volker and Dick Richmond

OroQuest Press
St. Louis

Dedicated to Kenneth G. White Sr.,
who has done more to promote treasure
hunting than any other man in history.
We owe him a great debt.

Also by Roy Volker and Dick Richmond:

TREASURE UNDER YOUR FEET
Adventurers' Handbook of Metal Detecting

Roy Volker with some of the coins he found on a Florida beach.
(Dick Richmond Photo)

TABLE OF CONTENTS

IN THE WAKE OF THE GOLDEN GALLEONS

A narrative by Roy Volker

as told to Dick Richmond

1

A GOLDEN GALLEON

*C*APTAIN MATIAS DE ORELLANA *stood on the deck of his galleon,* Nuestra Senora de la Maravillas, *peering into the mist. A thousand yards off the stern he could make out the vague shape of the galleon* Jesus Marie. *About the same distance off the port bow was the capitana or the flagship of the Marquis de Montlealgre. The rest of the fleet was hidden in the dimness.*

Dawn did not break on January 4, 1656; day simply came into existence. It was dark and gradually it grew light enough to be called gray.

As morning became afternoon, the oppressive gloom never changed. It was the kind of day that makes a person moody and reflective.

Not that Orellana was a very introspective individual. It was just that the weather and the area in which they were sailing made him think about death; his death.

Sudden squalls would strike and then just as suddenly disappear. They were more a nuisance than a danger, yet they kept the seas in the Straits of Florida choppy. The wind always seemed to be blowing in the direction opposite to that of the current, which created great swells that bounced the 650-ton treasure galleon around like a cork.

The 150-foot Maravillas *looked more like a floating high-rise than a ship, and that's the way she handled. At her best, the galleon was not a seaman's dream, and she was far from being at her best. She was a worm-eaten, leaky tub and long before the treasure was loaded aboard, Orellana had warned the pompous Marquis of her condition.*

The Marquis, however, was no seaman. He had obtained his commission as the captain-general of the fleet because he was a friend of the king. So when Orellana made his report, the Marquis regarded the captain's words as a sign of weakness. He let Orellana know the king was impatient for his gold and would tolerate no delays.

Orellana was made aware, too, he could maintain his command or give it up; it mattered not to the Marquis. Whatever, the Maravillas *would sail whether Orellana or someone else was in charge.*

Giving up his command had never entered Orellana's mind. Not only did he not want to be considered a coward, he had no intention of losing the rewards of carrying such a vast treasure. His share of the 5,000,000 pesos* in gold and silver would be a small fortune and Orellana was not about to be cheated by the high-handed methods of this lap dog of Charles IV.

Orellana did not complain again even when more passengers were permitted to make the voyage aboard the Maravillas *than he considered wise. More than 700 sailors, soldiers and civilians were jammed onto the vessel. He had commanded overcrowded, leaky ships between the New World and Spain before. A few died of diseases during a voyage, a few would die this time. That was inevitable and it did not concern him.*

What did concern him were things he knew were there but couldn't see. The waters between Havana and Bermuda were ship-killers filled with reefs and sandbanks that would rip the bottom out of a vessel. Hundreds of others had gone to their deaths on that stretch and Orellana did not intend for the Maravillas *to join them.*

Because of the roughness of the water only sailors were on deck, which was best for everyone. The hands needed no one cluttering the way.

Without exception everyone else was below, most of them seasick. The smell was as evil as the day, but for those who had exhausted their stomach fluids it didn't matter. They were insensitive to everything but their own pain. Many would have preferred death to the suffering they were enduring. They would get their wish.

Orellana was having his own problems. Before dawn the Maravillas *was having to tack in an attempt to maintain its northeasterly course. By late afternoon the wind had picked up and the current began to run in strength toward the shoals.*

Being a veteran seaman, the captain could have handled that. What brought him to near panic was the sudden premature darkening of the sky to the northeast. A veil of black fog was moving ominously toward his ship. He knew what it was and didn't waste time staring at it. Turning to his second in command, he snapped orders to bring the ship around so that her prow would be cutting the wind. There was no time to bring the ship about so they could run with the storm; the best he could hope for was to head directly into it.

If they had been away from the shoals, Orellana wouldn't have

*A peso was about an ounce.

worried too much. However, they were not in the open sea and knowing that created a surge of emotion in him that flooded his mind with foreboding. He knew his future, could see it, and the knowledge sent terror racing through his entire body.

What Orellana saw in his mind's eye were the shallow subterranean sandbanks that were going to swallow his ship. He and the rest would be buried under the sea miles from any point of land.

The screaming, unseen horrors of the blackness were approaching and he tried to shut them out of his mind. Men were sent up the lines, others were taking soundings with lead weights, most of the rest were passing orders from mouth to ear in an effort to overcome the noise of death's howling voice.

However, the veil shrouded the ship almost before Orellana realized it. In an instant it masked the Marquis's capitana and then the Maravillas *was in it. It wasn't over yet, but it wouldn't be long, and ironically it wouldn't be the shoals that would kill the* Maravillas *but the capitana.*

Hours passed like minutes in the bone-wearing fight for life aboard the treasure ship. No matter what was done, however, control belonged to the sea and the wind, and it was that combination that brought the capitana and the Maravillas *together in what was to be the climax for the* Maravillas.

When the ships collided, the capitana suffered some damage, but the Maravillas *was dealt a mortal blow. She was left crippled and out of control.*

Water gushed through the hole that the Marquis's ship punched in her hull. She began to list and moments later Orellana heard the crunch of splitting timbers as a reef tore away part of his ship's bottom. Almost before the first crash was over, the galleon had slammed into a sandbank and began to turn on her side.

Cannons broke loose and slid across the decks crushing everything and everyone in their way. Below, the screams of men and women were muffled by the screams of others and of the sea pouring in to claim them for its own. Some awakened just in time to have their mouths and lungs filled with salt water. Others died without awakening.

The Maravillas *capsized. When she did, some of the sailors were thrown into the ocean. The galleon sank and was quickly covered in part by the sandbank. About fifty of the 700 survived. Orellana was not one of them. The sea had claimed another prize; this time a rich one.*

§   §   §

My introduction to the *Maravillas* wasn't quite so dramatic. What I had was some research from the Archives of the Indies in Seville relating to the galleon's manifest, and to the attempts of the Spaniards to recover the millions she was carrying, attempts that spanned several decades.

The story of what may have happened on January 4, 1656, was pieced together over a period of several years in which I searched for this great sunken treasure. At first it was just another wreck and as I examined the documents, I had no idea that she would occupy so much of my life. Neither did I know I would come so very close to finding her, and then lose her to someone else when she was within my grasp.

I remember looking at the papers in my hands and seeing a reference to a place called Los Mimbres. The problem with the location was that Los Mimbres seemed to be everywhere . . . and nowhere.

There were several references to the location in the research, yet there was no Los Mimbres on modern charts. Suppositions based on other suppositions placed it at Conch Key in the Florida Keys, and at three areas of the Bahamas — Red Riding Rocks, Cay Sal Bank and Memory Rock.

If this were a story of failure, it probably wouldn't be worth relating. However, the chase after the *Maravillas* was filled with successes, not only in the treasure found but in the direction it gave my life. For those who wonder why men will undergo danger and privation in pursuit of a rainbow, perhaps this will explain how it can happen.

—ROY VOLKER

2

ON THE WRONG SIDE OF AN ANGRY CANNON

I T WAS HAROLD STILL WHO BROUGHT THE RESEARCH ON the *Maravillas* back from Spain. He had traveled to the archives as we were forming World Wide Treasure Research in the early 1960s. By the time we became interested in working the galleon, Harold and I were the only ones remaining of the original group. One by one the others had dropped away.

Bill Settlemoir, the man who originated the idea for a treasure-hunting company, was the first to go; Art Hartman, who could build anything and who could make himself be almost anything except a follower, was next; then it was George Traber, the seaman who tired of being the captain of a ship of fools.

Harold was our organizer and researcher, our contact man with government officials and our electronics man. He would depart in a short time as well because of his family. I had a wife and a family, too, but situations affect each person differently. However, as we scanned the list of the *Maravillas* treasure, he thought he had his hand on the handle of a pot of gold and had no intention of letting go.

At the time I had none of the talents of the others. I still can't build anything. I wasn't even a particularly good diver, and my experience with treasure hunting was almost entirely on land. I had been the fund raiser for the group, and because it had been me who had sold the idea to the investors in World Wide, the company became my responsiblity. There was no escaping it.

And so began the great rainbow chase. Many would join it for a time, then tire and fall off the pace. How it started seems logical in retrospect, yet as a poor kid growing up in St. Louis during the Depression I had a firm grip on reality. I knew what fantasy was, and that the pirate gold of ''Treasure Island'' was nothing but myth.

Volker with a chest found in the Bahamas and with a silver bar and several silver ingots found off the Florida coast in 1965.

(Renyold Ferguson Photo)

The obverse and reverse sides of the 1715 eight escudo Spanish Golden Royal, which New York coin auctioneer Hans M. F. Schulman has valued at between $50,000 and $75,000. The coin was found by Roy Volker on a Florida beach after a storm.

(Larry Williams Photos)

In the '30s reality was a 7 a.m. to 7 p.m. job in a factory for $10 a week, loaded dice and a marked deck of cards, learning to hit the guy with the chip on his shoulder before he hit you. There were other realities like the con games, the punks who looked for fame and dames with a gun and a sock loaded with BBs, the girls who got their three squares a day the hard way, at two dollars a throw.

It all seemed normal. Most of those people never had enough to eat. The big ambition for a lot of the kids in my neighborhood was to own a grocery. That wasn't for me.

I was already thinking about that pot of gold, and I thought I could get it with my hands. Now before anyone gets the wrong impression, I don't want you to think I meant to work with my hands. I intended to be a gambler or a prize fighter. In a small way I became both, but not before I received my introduction to the sea in the Navy in World War II.

As introductions go, I've had better. From the beginning I knew my military life was going to be strenuous. Initially, however, it didn't seem so bad. As a matter of fact, it occurred to me I could be in training for a career as a radio operator.

There was a hitch to that of course because the training I was receiving was as a radio operator with an amphibious force. I didn't know what amphibious meant, but I was aware it had nothing to do with programming for Jack Benny or Bob Hope. When I found out, I had a severe attack of indigestion.

Just when I was getting used to the idea, I was transferred to Fort Pierce, Florida, where I was suddenly being taught how to capture towns in an outfit called scouts and raiders.

Amphibious is a big word; the meaning of scouts and raiders I understood. I had heard scuttlebutt about my new tent-mates. They were the Navy's and the Army's elite infiltration forces, commandos who would sneak into enemy territory and take over installations and create havoc to pave the way for invasions.

On paper it all sounded very heroic, but the way I understood it, those words meant we were to be right in the middle and everyone would be shooting at us. The good and the bad are all ugly from that point of view.

The outfit was comprised mostly of athletes, and I had been an amateur boxer before the war. That may be the reason I had been tapped. However, I'll never know.

Not that it matters today. In fact, it really didn't matter then. No sooner had I finished training than I was once again unexpectedly and inexplicably reassigned. I was plucked from my tent and placed in a hotel in the middle of Fort Pierce. My job was a radio shack in town.

I could not believe my good luck. Harold Still always said I had the greatest luck in the world. Maybe that was the reason he turned World Wide over to me when I finally joined the field operation in Florida.

World Wide was twenty years in the future in World War II. Yet it was right there at Fort Pierce that I received my first whiff of sunken Spanish gold No one knew it at the time but a few hundred feet offshore were millions of dollars in treasure mixed in with the bones of a fleet that sank in a hurricane on July 31, 1715.

However, in 1943 my only concern was making the best of a great situation. I pretended to be a wall so no one would notice me. For about two months no one did. Then, there I was in the South Pacific aboard a landing craft moving in on beaches occupied by serious people shooting at me. Two landing craft were blown out from under me.

In the Pacific I received my first peek at what was under the waves; I mean not counting the times the landing craft and I parted company abruptly. Everything in the war zone was not beachheads. There was plenty of peaceful moments and even a would-be gambler couldn't spend all his time throwing dice against a bulkhead.

Yet on those marvelous islands most of the liberty belles looked like coconuts with eyes. In spite of that, beach time was the best and I used to try my hand at fishing with the natives. It was from one of those native fishermen I obtained my first pair of goggles, crude things that didn't completely seal out the water.

With them I received my first look underwater without my vision being blurred. I saw fish that didn't seem afraid of me, and coral formations so beautiful I was reluctant to take my face out of the water.

My excitement must have been obvious because the native who had taken me out in his boat sat grinning at me. I remember him vividly because all his front teeth were missing and as he smiled, he sucked his lips into his mouth. I spent the afternoon with him and by the end of the day he had my wristwatch and I had his goggles.

It was one of the best trades I ever made. Not because it turned me into a diver but because the goggles served me so well. I used them every chance I had and when I wasn't using them, my shipmates were — on an hourly basis. I was really raking in the money until some smart aleck on a tender rented them for a couple of hours so he could make copies to sell.

When the war ended, that was the last of my skin diving for a long while. As yet, I had not attempted scuba. That was to come.

In the late '40s I became a professional prize fighter and a part-time uranium prospector. A busted hand ended my ring career prematurely, the disappointment of finding a quarter-of-a-million-dollar deposit of uranium and not being able to bring it out of the wilderness caused me to give up searching for a time. When I returned to prospecting, it was in search of gold, not uranium.

With the hope of my winning that big purse as a boxer over, I settled into a 9-to-5 job. I don't think I really ever expected to make a strike in the gold fields; it was just something to do to soothe the restlessness that has burdened me all my life.

The only time I was able to go searching was on vacations and that wasn't enough. The 9-to-5 syndrome was getting to me. I needed something else.

It was during a period of extreme restlessness that I met Art Hartman. He was tall and boyishly thin then. His light brown hair was short and his dress casual yet in good taste. What I remember about that first meeting was that he was a story-teller who had a contagious way of laughing at his own words. He didn't always talk; just when he had something to say, or when he thought the time was ripe for a joke. His basic sense of humor could turn an uncomfortable moment into a good time, which made him a fine companion. What was more important was he had a point of view similar to mine, which eventually made him a friend.

When we met, we were both deer hunting on a farm near Ste. Genevieve, Missouri. For years deer hunting to me was a sport of carrying a gun and doing little to disturb the peace of the wildlife. Then one day I was complaining to an old man about my bad luck.

"Never shoot anything, do you?" he asked.

"No," I confessed.

"Climb a tree," he told me.

I looked at him in dismay, sure he was putting me on.

"That's right," he said. "Find a deer run and then climb a tree and wait. You'll have them coming right up to you."

I nodded, not believing a word of what he said, and went about my merry way of trying to keep my feet from freezing. When I returned empty handed once again, the old man said, "Climb a tree."

The next morning I was up in a tree at dawn. Just as the sun broke a great stag walked right under me to be sure I wouldn't miss him. I was so proud of that first kill I think I was still smiling when I went to sleep that night.

At any rate, that is how I have been hunting deer ever since. And that is where Art first saw me . . . up a tree.

"What you doing up in the tree?" he asked.

"Deer hunting," I said.

I could hear him laughing as he disappeared from view. In fact, he was still laughing when I returned to cabin that afternoon, and stopped only when he saw the stag I had bagged. Then it was my turn to laugh.

Art is a quick learner and the following day he was in a tree, too. By the time deer-hunting season came around again, he had built himself a blind in the trees that made hunting comfortable as well as productive. Art never did anything halfway if he could do it correctly.

Hunting would take us into some pretty wild country, but not nearly as wild or as dangerous as when we went into the mountains of Montana and Wyoming in search of gold.

Art, too, was a man seeking adventure, only he was doing it in a different way. Art had taken up skydiving and he drove stock cars for the Midwest Racing Association. For my part, I don't like airplanes even when they are on the ground; there is no way in the world I would ever jump out of one. To me stock car racing seemed like war.

Even Art gave up racing for a time. It stopped after an incident at the Belle-Clair Speedway in Belleville, Illinois, in 1955.

He was racing on the final lap for the finish line when a 1937 Ford smashed into another car just in front of him. The force of the impact was so great the Ford pushed the first car up against an eighteen-foot-high retaining wall. Art didn't have time to turn. When he hit the wreckage, which had formed a ramp, his car flew up and over the wall, making a 360-degree turn in the air. The car landed on its wheels and Art emerged unhurt, but his wife, who was pregnant at the time, thought he had been killed and fainted. They lost the baby.

I admired Art's daring, even when I thought it was stupid, yet it was his ability with his hands that really engendered my esteem. His formal education is as limited as my own. In spite of his occasional misuse of the English language and sometimes frustrating single-mindedness, he is a talented builder of things. What's more he never has to be shoved to do them.

Give Art a problem and he will solve it, a challenge and he will meet it, a goal and he will run for it, as long as he is in charge. That was to be the source of his conflict with World Wide, and the reason he abruptly left the company he had worked so hard to form.

That, too, was in the future. When we met, being in charge had no relevancy. Not only did we share a sense of adventure but we had common interests in hunting, fishing and diving.

Art was self-taught in scuba, yet he was accomplished enough to instruct a class at the YMCA in St. Louis. He was one of the first instructors in the Midwest, and had formed diving clubs and associations. St. Louis acquired its first recompression chamber through his efforts. He was also a dealer in scuba supplies. I became one of his students.

A deliberate man, Art is the kind who makes a fine teacher. The first night in his class he let me sample what it was like to be able to breathe underwater, and I was hooked. Friendship or no friendship, I had to go through the entire course routine just like everyone else.

After eight weeks the rest of the class and I were taken out for our first open-water dive in a little lake near Steelville, Missouri. It was April, and cold, and the water was murky. This was definitely not the clear, pleasantly warm water of the South Pacific. The whole situation began to seem a little flaky to me.

Watching Art and the others don their wet suits, I felt I had no choice but to follow. I began to think about Art jumping out of air-planes and driving like hell in competition with a bunch of nuts around those dirt race tracks. I mean, he did those things just for fun. I glanced at the water, then watched Art slip over the side of the boat.

He smiled at me, and I may have smiled back, but if I did, it was twisted. It has something to do with a conflict between face and brain. Brain was saying this is stupid and face was trying to agree.

Yet, a moment later, I found myself in the water following Art to the bottom. In truth, I don't know whether I followed him to the bottom or not. I couldn't see a thing after I was two feet beneath the surface. Like a fool, though, I headed down, arms at my sides, flippers moving in perfect form, past the thermocline* and straight into the mud at the bottom.

That was it. Straight down. Straight up. My first open-water dive in scuba lasted one minute. I lifted myself into the boat and washed the muck from hands, head and face mask.

As I was cleaning up, Art surfaced and flipped over to the boat and asked, "What do you think, Roy?"

This time face and brain were in complete agreement. There wasn't a smile between the two of them. I said, "I've had enough diving for the day." What I really wanted to say was, "I've had enough diving . . . period!"

The rest of the day I sat in the boat and watched Art and the others enjoying themselves in that mud bath. I felt like an idiot just being there. Diving in the ocean was great, but this . . .

It was a month before Art talked me into trying it again. Art was a dealer in AMF Voit scuba products and we were to be joined at Table Rock Lake in the Ozarks by Harold Still, a friend of Art's who was employed by the Voit company.

From everything Art told me about Harold, I think I knew him before I met him. "Harold is a college man," Art said, "a former naval officer, a super scuba diver. Roy, you'll like him. He's a little nuts."

That was high praise indeed from Art, and the way he went on and on about him, I knew he wanted me to like him.

As it turned out, the conflict for leadership in World Wide was between those two, which seems incredible even now. Yet people change when situations change.

Art grinned like a hound at a barbecue when he saw Harold and I had hit it off. It was easy to like Harold because he was everything Art had said he was, and more. Harold had one of those captivating grins that wins over anyone he wants on his side. Everyone, however, is not selected for that privilege.

When we arrived at Table Rock, Harold was there waiting for us. Again the water was murky, but I suited up regardless and dove with them. I figured if Art had given Harold the big build-up to me, he had returned the favor in my case, and I didn't want Harold thinking that this former professional prize fighter was chicken.

As I entered the water, I thought how silly it was for me to try to prove to someone I didn't know I was something I really wasn't. Yet I went, moving along the bluffs looking for carp with a spear gun. Having carp to search for gave me something to think about

*The thermocline is the point at which a layer of warm water rests on a layer of much colder water.

other than myself. The claustrophobia I had felt on my first sixty-second plunge did not bother me this time.

As I finned along with Art and Harold, I seemed to be getting the hang of it when I spotted a fish. I turned and the fish was gone. When I turned back, Art and Harold were gone. Lonely is suddenly being underwater by yourself. Right then I really did miss those two guys . . . and I had just met Harold.

Surfacing, I found the spot where their bubbles were breaking the surface. Diving straight down, I rejoined them. "Good thinking," I said to myself. "You're on the way to becoming a lake diver." Of course, I still didn't know why I wanted to be a lake diver, or any kind of a diver for that matter.

I didn't shoot any carp that day. Art got a couple big ones. Harold . . . well, Harold shot some, but his average wasn't too great. Regardless, it was a good day.

The following several weekends were spent at the lake. We enjoyed being together and with the passing months our friendship grew.

Bill Settlemoir was my friend. At the time he owned a small roofing company in St. Louis. He's a little guy compared to Art, Harold and myself. What he lacks in size, he makes up for in big ideas, and he was no exception then.

He and Art got along well, but there was some small barrier between Bill and Harold, mainly because Bill would baffle Harold with baloney. Then just as Harold thought he had Bill trapped in his own words, Bill would lay it out for him just as he said it was and grin.

As you are already aware, Bill became the fourth member of our group. When he did, things began to happen. None of us, except Bill, have been the same since.

It all seemed innocent enough when it started. Art was to appear at the St. Louis Sports Show, representing Voit. Harold, Bill and I offered to help. Then one evening before the show closed its ten-day run, Bill suggested the four of us pool our money and go on a treasure hunt in Florida or in the Bahamas.

Harold's response was to laugh. I just told Bill he was nuts. But Art didn't think so. You have to remember Art was also a skydiver and a race car driver. I thought, "He would!"

Later that evening, I noticed Bill swaying Harold with convincing conversation and before the night was over Harold was ready to go. On top of that he, Art and Bill ganged up on me before I really knew what was happening. The three of them were making plans to hire a boat. My vote was counted; I was going.

Within a few months we had arranged for a boat, the *Virg a Lona,* with George Traber as our captain. Traber was everything a seaman should be: big, cocky, smart about the ocean, afraid of nothing. With him, we had all the elements we needed for World Wide. At this point in our experience, if there was to be a treasure-hunting outfit, only Bill Settlemoir knew about it, and he wasn't talking — yet.

Traber had his fifty-eight-foot, twin-diesel vessel moored at Marathon, Florida. We rented a trailer in St. Louis to haul our equipment and drove there.

The day we arrived we cast off for a small group of coral islands called Cay Sal Bank, about twenty-five miles off the coast of Cuba. That was one of the areas thought to be the Los Mimbres of the *Maravillas*. Years later I would return there, but not for Orellana's galleon. I would return at the head of an expedition sponsored by the National Enquirer, in which psychic David Hoy would attempt to find sunken ships by extrasensory perception.*

At this time, in our just-budding interest in undersea treasure hunting, we had no idea where to begin looking for wrecks. Cay Sal Bank is in the old Bahama Channel, which had been used on some of the early voyages by the Spanish. Traber had heard of wrecks there.

Later all of us would learn the importance of research, wreck identification, electronics, organization and the business of running a treasure-salvage operation. Right then we were only four lake divers off on an adventure. If our captain knew where there were wrecks, that was good enough for us. If the wreck was old, then it stood to reason there had to be treasure.

Only now do I realize how ridiculous the whole idea was. If we found a wreck, we couldn't have done a thing with it. Locating a wreck is one thing; digging it out from under sand and coral is something else. Besides, we had nothing with which to dig.

I suppose every group has to start somewhere, but usually someone has at least a little experience. We were the Keystone Kops underwater. Eagerness was the only thing we had going for us, and that was far outweighed by our tremendous ignorance.

Anchoring off a small island, we suited up and I jumped over the stern. When I hit the water, I entered like Dumbo, arms and legs and ears akimbo, making a big splash. As the bubbles began to clear, I caught a flash of something black moving toward me. Before I could see what it was, I was out of the water yelling that the place was full of sharks.

Bill and Art ran to the stern. Just as they got there, Harold surfaced. Harold had put on a tank and had already been in the water when I went over the side. What I had glimpsed was Harold in his black wet suit, not a shark.

I grinned sheepishly. Art and Bill smiled in sympathy. There was no sympathy with George Traber, however. He rolled on the deck roaring with laughter. Pointing a finger at me, he gasped out a word at a time. I didn't want to hear, yet I knew what he was saying.

"That's the first time," he gurgled , "I've ever seen anyone walk on water."

*An account of the voyage appeared in the October 28, 1973, issue of the National Enquirer.

George had a rough sense of humor, and I liked him for it, but not right then. The incident had destroyed my morning and he wasn't doing a thing to improve it.

In the days that followed it was Harold who watched over Bill and me. He wanted to make sure we were safe. Whenever we would swim off by ourselves, I would see him watching, and pretty soon he would be there with us. Years later Harold would tell me something I have valued since. It was after I returned from the West Indies.

"Roy, you're a different man in the water," he said.

It wasn't much, yet from Harold it was high praise.

George Traber was to become important to the four of us when we finally did form a treasure-hunting outfit. We eventually would buy the *Virg a Lona* and hire him as captain. He knew his boat and the ocean and he was one of the better free divers in Florida.

The water was beautifully clear and it was George who came up with a workable suggestion as to how we might find a wreck. Since we had no detecting equipment to enable us to locate a buried wreck under sand in shallow water, we would eyeball search by being pulled on a sled behind the boat in areas that were mostly hardpan. Hardpan is ocean bottom where there isn't much sand and he thought the place for that would be in slightly deeper water.

George had used the sled in searching for lobster. Guiding it was simple. A diver could make it go up or down with a handle that controlled the rudder. If he found something, he simply dropped off and the boat would turn around to pick him up. This can be a dangerous system if someone doesn't happen to see you drop off.

In a week of dragging a diver behind the boat we found two wrecks — one modern and one with a small ballast* pile. Neither produced anything. We planned staying and working several more days, but that was to change quickly. The Bay of Pigs was a recent memory at the time and we were too close to Cuba as far as the United States Coast Guard was concerned. Where was the Coast Guard when we needed it a few years later when the *Virg a Lona* went aground in Cuban waters?

We had been at Cay Say about a week when one morning a Coast Guard plane circled us for a few minutes, then disappeared. Just before noon a Coast Guard cutter appeared over the horizon and pulled alongside.

I could see the crew running around the deck, which gave me an uneasy feeling. I was much too familiar with the call to battle stations. Then when the gun turret on the forward deck swung around and leveled at us, I was sick. I couldn't imagine what we had done to warrant this kind of reception.

A loud horn sounded: "Stand by for boarding."

I was relieved to see an officer and three coast guardmen in a dingy headed out way. Compared to the cannon leveled at us, the

*Ballast stones were used in old ships to keep them stable in the water.

.45 automatic strapped to the officer's hip and the submachine guns being carried by two of the men seemed friendly. Also, I knew at least they were going to talk before they started shooting.

George was belligerent. I couldn't believe it.

"They have guns, George!"

"Screw 'em. We haven't done anything."

"We don't have to have done anything, George. They have guns."

"I've had trouble with these guys before. They're just lookin' for somethin' to do."

The dingy pulled alongside and the officer and the men climbed aboard. The officer demanded to know what we were doing so close to Cuba.

"Searchin' for wrecks," George told him.

As the men combed the *Virg a Lona,* the officer advised George we would do much better to leave the area.

"We're not in Cuban waters," George snapped.

"If you stay," the officer warned, "you might find yourself in trouble."

The officer had such a way with words . . . and with cannons . . . we decided Florida might be a better place to hunt.

Over George's objection we hauled anchor and headed back for Marathon. Once underway, however, it occurred to George he knew of a wreck at Looe Key. The key was named after the *H.M.S. Looe,* a forty-gun frigate, which was under the command of Captain Ashby Uting when it sank after striking a reef at night on February 5, 1744. At the time it sank it had been towing a captured Spanish ship called the *Snow.*

The *Looe* was discovered in 1950 by Art McKee and other divers in the Keys. However, no one has yet found the *Looe's* prize. In the late 1960s an unidentified French ship was uncovered nearby. The man who was to find it was Art Hartman.

Yet, when we were there, Art was just another talented beginner and we were all looking forward to seeing the wreck with the same eagerness.

The *Looe* was against the reef in eighteen feet of water. Over the years some of the cannons had been removed by divers, but we were at least seeing a wreck with something on it. George anchored the *Virg a Lona* right over the ballast pile.

The *Looe* is a fun wreck on which to pick, but it is far from being a treasure wreck. A wreck in tropical waters is nothing more than a pile of rubble, unless it is modern and made of metal or in very deep water where the terado worms that eat the wood cannot live. A good wreck site isn't even that because it's buried. If a wreck is exposed, a treasure hunter has to assume it has been picked over by other divers.

The first day on the *Looe* we picked up drift pins and iron spikes, cannon balls and several pellets of lead grapeshot. Art found several pieces of pottery and an unbroken bottle. It was Harold who uncovered our first piece of treasure, a Spanish copper coin. We were fanning the bottom with our hands. It was slow and tiring, but we were finding things.

En route to Marathon after the first day back, Art decided that we could probably do better if we had an airlift. An airlift is an undersea vacuum and Art was sure he could build one. He had never touched an airlift before but had seen one in a movie.

"Will it work?" I asked as he was building it.

"How the heck should I know?" Art responded.

As he was putting the airlift together, he explained how it was supposed to function. All of us, including George, stood around watching and listening as if we were school children being taught our first lesson in basic treasure equipment.

Art drilled a hole near the end of a long, four-inch thinwall aluminum pipe. Through the hole he placed a fitting to which he attached a rubber garden hose.

"The compressor on deck forces air down through the hose," Art explained. "When it reaches the pipe here at the bottom, the air, which is now compressed because of the pressure, has to escape. It rushes up through the pipe, causing a vacuum, which should suck up the sand off the bottom. Theoretically, the deeper you go, the more the pressure and the greater the vacuum."

It performed just the way he had said it would. As a matter fact, a ten-inch airlift he built a few years later worked so well we couldn't control it.

Compared to the methods available today for uncovering a wreck, that four-inch airlift was a pretty primitive tool. Yet, with it we uncovered more in the first half hour of digging than we had the entire day before.

More cannon balls were found, broken pottery, broken bottles, a copper teakettle, a bosun's whistle and several broken clay pipes. On one of the pipes was stamped "Liverpool England."

Stopping for lunch, we were back at it in the afternoon. I found several buttons and another pipe. About the end of the day Harold uncovered another copper coin about the size of a quarter. It was badly worn and there was no date on it. However, we were able to make out that it was French.

We congratulated ourselves for finding this grand collection of junk. All we had done was move in on a well-known wreck that had been picked on for years. We thought we were really doing something. Nothing to this treasure hunting, we said. That saying about ignorance being bliss is more than correct.

Any fool could do it. With that I have no argument. Time after time we went out of our way to prove the point. But then why should I spoil the book for you; you'll find out soon enough.

A diver uses an airlift to clear the sand from a wreck at Cay Sal Island, just north of Cuba, July 1973. It was one of two wrecks found.
(Don Paule Photo)

3

HOW TO SINK A SHIP

THE *LOOE*, AS IT TURNED OUT, was a great learning experience for all of us. My lesson started as soon as George Traber said he knew of a ship called the *Looe* at Looe Key. Even I could figure out that if one key was named after a sunken ship then there were probably more named the same way. The idea stimulated me to search for clues, which was my introduction to research. For the treasure hunter research is indispensible. George taught me a lesson and I was about to teach him one. The difference was the lesson I taught him caused him to lose some sleep.

When the Coast Guard chased us away from Cay Sal Bank, it was past noon. By the time we got underway another hour or so had gone by. So when night fell, we were still at sea.

George turned to me and asked, "Roy, do you know how to run a compass course?"

"No problem," I responded, grinning. "I was in the Navy."

Thus assured, George immediately joined the others, who had already fallen asleep. The first thing I discovered about the *Virg a Lona* was she had too much play in the wheel. In trying to maintain a bearing, I was scooting the boat all over the place. My wakes looked like figure eights. However, there was no one awake to see what I was doing. So what if it takes us a little longer to get there, I decided.

Concentrating on what I was doing, I almost missed seeing the light off our starboard bow. When I finally did see it, I was fascinated because it was getting larger and larger. The larger the light got, the rougher the water. I had to have a correlation, but I had not figured it out before George awakened and shouted at me.

The light I was watching so intently was on the stern of a large

Divers swim across an area with the scatterings of a wreck to photograph it.

(Don Paule Photo)

freighter. We were riding in her wake and it was like being on a roller coaster.

"For crying out loud, Roy,"George snapped, pushing me roughly away from the wheel. "I thought you said you were in the Navy."

"I was a radioman," I admitted.

George regarded me with malice and grumbled something I would just as soon keep to myself. After that he stayed awake. It was the only time I was allowed to pilot the boat on that voyage.

We did not travel to Florida just because we knew the water was clear. We did not know much, but we did know the reefs of the Bahamian islands and those along the Florida coast were littered with wrecks.

For the 300 years that Spain controlled the Caribbean, gold and silver from Mexico and from South America and trade goods from the Orient were being shipped back to Europe. The routes were well-established because of the prevailing trade winds.

Leaving Spain, the ships would sail to the Canaries, then to the Windward Islands in the West Indies. The galleons that were to pick up the gold and silver from the mines in South America would sail on to Cartegena and Porto Bello. Others would sail to Vera Cruz in Mexico. There the gold and silver of Mexico would be stowed aboard the ships as well as merchandise from the Orient, which had been transported across the Pacific on the Manila galleons.

The Manila galleons put in at Acapulco. From there the pottery, silks, spices, ivory, jade and all the other precious commodities of the Far East would be shipped by mule train overland to the Gulf of Mexico.

The ships would then sail up the Gulf of Mexico and down Florida's west coast. They would rendezvous in Havana and from there set sail for Spain in fleets.

The fleet system was designed for protection against the pirates who infested the waters as well as against Spain's European neighbors. It didn't take long for England, France and Holland to decide they, too, wanted a piece of the action.

Yet the real danger to ships of Spain was not their human foes. It was a combination of bureaucracy at its worst, and the weather. The kings of Spain were twenty per centers. To make sure they received their fifth, they established a maritime bureau called La Casa de Contratacion. The Casa had its busy and almost totally ignorant fingers into everything involving shipping, from what was to be carried aboard which ships to how the captains were to fight their battles if attacked.

One might think there was some sanity connected with this procedure until he learned the closest most of those bureaucrats of the Casa ever came to the sea was downtown Seville or Cadiz.

With such a system everyone was out to beat it. Wholesale cheating became established practice. The manifest of a ship seldom, if ever, listed all the treasure aboard. One of the best examples of this was *Nuestra Senora de la Concepcion,* a 680-ton galleon that sank in 1641 on a reef in the Bahamas called Abreojos.

Today the reef is called Silver Bank because of the vast amount of silver an American, Sir William Phips, recovered from the wreck in 1687. Phips removed almost twice the amount of silver listed on the manifest.

Phips, I was to learn in the last year of my search for the *Maravillas,* had stopped to pick on the bones of Orellana's galleon in 1681. If I would have known that when Harold returned from Spain with the research, it might have provided me with the one vital clue I had been missing before.

While Spain's European neighbors were building sleeker and faster ships, Spain stuck with its top-heavy construction. The Spanish were good soldiers, but when it came to the sea they never quite caught on. For example, it was the captain-general who was in charge of the fleets and not the admiral as I had mentioned earlier regarding the Marquis de Montlealgre, who commanded the 1656 plate fleet at the time of the disaster.

The ships were leaky and worm-eaten. They were difficult to steer and navigation was crude to say the least. Not only was navigation poor, but the navigators guarded their secrets zealously, even from one another. In some businesses it is known as protecting a good gig.

At best, those ships were in the hands of nature, and nature is capricious. The fleets would sail from Havana up the Florida Straits, using its current to carry them to about Cape Canaveral. At the Cape they would catch the wind that hopefully would blow them to Bermuda and Spain.

Of the thousands of ships that sank in those 300 years, most went down in storms and in shallow water. Almost the entire 1715 fleet sank in a hurricane on the Florida coast between Fort Pierce and Sebastian Inlet. In another storm in 1733 a plate fleet went down in the Florida Keys.

So our little group knew it was in the right haystack in which to find the golden needle. Yet searching for a needle in a dozen haystacks is easy compared to looking for a sunken and buried wreck in the sea when you do not know what you are doing.

I mentioned one of the two wrecks we found at Cay Sal Bank had a small ballast pile. The ballast the Spanish used was mostly round river stones, and that is what we saw there.

At Looe Key, however, the ballast consisted of large iron ingots, each weighing several hundred pounds. Bit by bit we were acquiring information about wreck identification. It was drawing us into the first stages of the treasure-hunting fever, a malady that has never left me.

4

S.E.C. — WHAT KIND OF A CLUB IS THAT?

THE IDEA FOR ESTABLISHING a treasure-hunting corporation did not occur to us at once. We spent months diving in lakes on weekends and reliving our adventure. Lake diving became boring and our days on the *Virg a Lona* became a well of memories from which we drew most of our conversation when together.

It was during this period that a big, rangy kid by the name of Dave Meinell joined us for a time. He was 6-foot-3, handsome and attractive to women of all shapes, sizes and ages. He was a natural diver who took to the water as if he had grown up on an island. When we met him, he was about to enter the Army. One day he would join World Wide and one of the first things he would do was to be interned in a Cuban prison with Harold Still.

Dave would sit around and listen to our conversation. He was a quiet kid, but occasionally he would add something to what was being said. One afternoon when we were discussing the *Looe* and the other wrecks we had found, he said, "That has to be the way a man wants to live."

None of us had said that before and we just kind of looked at one another and nodded. "Yeah," Bill Settlemoir agreed, "that has to be the way."

There was no conscious thought of pulling up roots by any of us as far as I knew. We were all family men with growing responsibilities. Each of us had a business or a career, and all of us were doing well.

Yet I found myself spending most of my free time in the first rudiments of research. Art was thinking of how to build a more efficient airlift. Either Bill or Harold, I don't remember which, investigated the type of search electronics available then.

22

In other words, mentally, all of us were ready when Bill suggested the corporation. What he said made sense. With a good boat, good electronics and enough money to sustain us for two years we would find plenty of treasure, enough for us to relax the rest of our lives.

Each of us was interested in having enough money to relax the rest of our lives. Yet what we talked about wasn't money. We had found an island called Water Cay, uninhabited except for birds and lizards. On one side of the island was a cove with a white sand beach and a reef that crawled out of the deep water right up to the shoreline. The reef was alive with fish of every color and description, with beauty as indescribable as a taste.

On the ocean side of Water Cay was a natural bridge that had been carved by the wind and the waves. Under the bridge the sea poured into a round grotto with a white sand bottom. As the water flowed through, it exited through caves that led to a bay of brilliant blue.

That's what we talked about, and the island with the abandoned lighthouse and the ruins of a small settlement. Cactus grew on that island, and three stubby palms.

Then there was Cay Sal Island with its rows of coconut palms, its untrammeled beaches and the small deep bay nestled at one end.

We talked about the sea and the wrecks and the thrill of swimming in the midst of schools of unfrightened fish. Touching what no one has touched, seeing what no one has seen, being where no one has been, those are the subjects covered by our words.

Sure treasure was important, and it became more so as we grew used to the unexpected. Yet it was all part of the same thing, of being absorbed by the great chase through the unexplored.

We purchased equipment: compressors for airlifting and for diving with hookah breathing devices,* diving gear. Art built airlifts of all sizes. Harold joined me in research, which became more intense. Art flew to Florida to discuss with George Traber the purchase of the *Virg a Lona.* George agreed to sell and to work with us for a salary plus a small percentage. At the same time we set out on the task of legally putting together a corporation.

Now all we needed was the money. It was Bill Settlemoir who came up with the idea of selling memberships in a treasure-hunting club. Could we legally do it?

"Sure," our lawyer advised us after consulting with some of his colleagues. His specialty incidentally was criminal law, not corporate law.

So we went ahead with the plan of setting up the Joint Adventures Treasure Investment Club. Brochures were printed explaining what we intended doing and how the splits were to be made. There were

---

*With a hookah a hose leads from the compressor to the diver's demand regulator, allowing a man to work on the bottom for long periods of time instead of having bottom time limited by the amount of air in his tank.

The original four as they dressed to promote an expedition by having potential investors join a club. The Securities and Exchange Commission put an immediate halt to that ill-advised enterprise. Photo is from the cover of their promotional brochure. From left: Art Hartman, Harold Still, Roy Volker and Bill Settlemoir.

five classes for investors, ranging from $5 to $1,000. We were to get half of anything found, the investors the other half. The division would be made on a percentage basis according to the amount of the original investment.

The sale took place at another St. Louis Sports Show. We made a display of artifacts and coins, and dressed in jackets with a large skull and crossbones on the front.

The first night of the show we had people standing in line to join our club. Money was pouring in so fast we were more worried about over-selling memberships than not having enough to accomplish what we intended to do.

The second night was better than the first, and the third started out with wall-to-wall people trying to push their money at us. From out of that crowd appeared a young man who identified himself as being with the S.E.C.

I smiled at him, wondering what kind of club the S.E.C. was. Within seconds I found out.

He explained that S.E.C. stood for Securities and Exchange Commission and suggested we stop selling memberships at once. The Commission, he further explained, interpreted our sale of memberships as a sale of securities.

"In my opinion," he said, "it appears you have been improperly advised. There will be no fine, as long as you return all the money you've collected. If you continue to sell memberships," he warned, "the Commission will take you to court and the fines will probably be more than you can afford."

The warning called for a five-minute conference by the officers of the Joint Adventures Treasure Investment Club. Unanimously we decided to postpone the sale until we could consult our attorney.

Bright and early the next morning the four of us were in our attorney's office. He was aghast. In seconds he was on the phone to discuss the situation with the colleagues who had given him the go-ahead. Each said they did not remember exactly what they had told him, but admitted it was possible they were in error.

An hour later our attorney was on his way to the airport for a flight to Jefferson City, Missouri, to consult with the S.E.C. people in the state capital. Just before the show that evening he called on the telephone to give us the bad news.

"The S.E.C. man was right," he said. "No more sales and you have to return the money."

Did you ever **have to** return money? No? Well, let me tell you we really did not know the kind of trouble we were in until we started to give it back.

At any rate, the next morning we were back in our attorney's office. He told us to forget his expenses and fees and offered to help if he could. I thought, "Good! Because now we're probably going to need a criminal lawyer."

We arranged a meeting with S.E.C. officials soliciting their advice as to how we might clear up the mess we were in. It seemed simple enough. We would write a check for the amount of each member's investment and send it along with a letter of explanation as to why we could not go ahead with the club as planned.

Returning the money became a problem because many of the members did not want to take their money back. Some thought we had found something and were trying to ease them out. Others were irritated with the S.E.C., which was only trying to protect them. They were going to stand on their rights and give us money even if we had to go to jail to prove a point.

Each of the recalcitrant ones had to be personally contacted and convinced that if he or she did not accept the check we sent, we would be in big trouble. It was months before the entire thing came to a conclusion.

Because of the bad advice, we were not only left without potential backing but were broke as well. The booth at the sports show had cost us, the brochures had cost us, and returning the money had really cost us.

That incident came close to curing us of gold fever. It probably would have, too, if Art had not received a call from George Traber in Florida. It seemed a group called Real Eight in a combined effort with Treasure Salvors was finding gold and silver coins on several wrecks between Sebastian Inlet and Fort Pierce. The greatest treasure find in history was on the verge of being discovered, which would lead to one of the stupidest gold rushes in history. It was there, but darn few persons were equipped to get at it.

Treasure Salvors had a pile of treasure, but the outfit did not want to sell it for fear of creating a stampede of treasure divers. Treasure Salvors, George informed Art, would sell us the rights to a wreck off Colored Beach five miles south of Fort Pierce for $30,000 because it needed working capital.

Art flew down and returned ten days later more excited than I had ever seen him before. "It's true," he bubbled. "The wreck is a winner and we can have it for thirty grand. Mel Fisher, who heads Treasure Salvors, said he'll help us get started and work with us for thirty days. After that we should know enough to handle the salvage operation ourselves ."

Our problem was a familiar one: Money. In the next two weeks I contacted everyone I knew trying to get backing. No one was interested in investing with four rainbow chasers.

Finally we had to contact Mel Fisher and tell him that we could not raise the cash. Again we were beaten. Even worse, we were being laughed at. A month later no one was laughing. Mel called me to say he had taken several gold disks and a pile of gold and silver coins off the wreck. Eventually Art and I would both be working for Fisher on those treasure wrecks. Art still later would run an operation that controlled the leases to all those wrecks. In that moment of defeat, however, that thought never entered our imaginations.

Mel was not trying to rub our noses in it; he just knew we would be interested. Shortly thereafter the wire services carried a story about Kip Wagner and his Real Eight Corporation, which had uncovered a galleon at Sebastian Inlet. They also reported that Treasure Salvors was bringing up piles of treasure from the wreck at Colored Beach.

It was at this point that Bill Settlemoir decided that his roofing and contracting business needed his full attention. We were again a threesome.

Treasure hunting lay in limbo for a long time after that, but eventually we took stock of our situation and decided to re-form. We needed a project. It was decided to send Harold to Spain to research a ship in Florida. Several weeks later Harold returned with a lot of information, including that on the *Maravillas*.

I'm not sure what was in my head at that stage of my life. In the years that have passed, I wondered why we continued to pursue the project. We believed in the pot of gold all right. Yet it went beyond that, and beyond the desire for adventure as well. As I examine my own motivations, I believe that the direction we were taking was based on friendship.

We had shared great times together, the greatest of which had been on the ocean treasure dive. I think we wanted to recapture that and keep it as long as we could. Unfortunately people can never bring back those moments that have grown so marvelous in their memories.

We thought we knew one another as only the best of friends can. That, in fact, was true as long as we didn't try to change our rather pedestrian life styles. When we transplanted ourselves into a hostile environment compared to the luxury and safety in St. Louis, we discovered we didn't even know ourselves much less one another.

We had no choice but to change and I think we resented it, and probably blamed one another for the problems that came with those changes. Consequently we became strangers to ourselves and to one another. Until the strangeness wore off, none of us was sure he liked the other persons. As it was, we had depended on one another's strengths and we had found us lacking.

World Wide Treasure Research was formed and incorporated in Florida on July 6, 1964. At the same time we applied for a search lease, and on August 19, 1964, the Internal Improvement Fund in Tallahassee granted World Wide the right to search for treasure in the offshore waters of Monroe County. The area ran from Miami to Key West.

Next, we tested and purchased a proton magnetometer, an instrument that detects gradients in the earth's magnetic field caused by local concentrations of ferrous material such as a shipwreck. The instrument was expensive, but we knew without it we would never be able to locate buried wrecks in deep or in shallow water.

Again investors were contacted, but this time we were selling stock in a legal corporation. We had a lease from the State of Florida, the twin-diesel *Virg a Lona,* divers and equipment. We also had done our research first and had a project. In fact, we might have made it work the way we had it structured except for two things: our lack of real understanding of the electronics and the capriciousness of the government officials calling the shots on treasure hunters from Tallahassee.

Our prospectus explained the obvious risks involved, and the entire program was fully outlined. Only well-to-do businessmen who could afford to take a flyer were contacted. It was a selling job and it was left mostly in my hands. Consequently, I was the one controlling the purse strings. That, in essence, is what eventually pulled me to the helm of the organization.

To raise the money needed took several months. As stock was being sold, Harold Still and Art Hartman divested themselves of everything they had in St. Louis, quit their jobs and moved to Florida to set up the operation. They moved too soon, which proved to be a mistake because they did it before we were financially ready.

Much of their first month in Florida was used in getting the *Virg a Lona* hauled. An office and a machine shop were set up in Key Largo.

It was winter and the weather was moving from one extreme to the other. Day after day our small group, which now included George Traber, was unable to do any searching. Heavy seas and strong winds kept the men on the beach.

When the weather finally did break, they started having problems with our magneto- meter. It would work one day and then would not function properly for a week at a time. The manufacturer was in Eur- ope. The head of the company was contacted and when we thought we had one problem solved, a new one would present itself.

Harold Still working on a fire pump on the Virg a Lona *in Florida.*
(Roy Volker Photo)

In desperation, Harold went looking for help and found a geophysicist from the University of Miami at Coral Gables who was willing to work on it. After weeks of tinkering and being unable to resolve the problem, it was decided to send the mag and the geophysicist to Europe so he would be there to see why the unit was malfunctioning.

Ten days and $1,000 later, the geophysicist returned shaking his head, saying the unit performed perfectly in Europe. That left us with the obvious conclusion: There was something screwed up in the magnetic field off the coast of Florida where we were searching. We were in an area at the tip of the mysterious Bermuda Triangle.* It made us wonder.

Finally, Art Hartman decided the magnetometer's sensing head might be the problem. We had not sent the head and cable to Europe along with the mag because they were so bulky.

Art worked on an experimental head all one night. Early the next morning it was tested near Key Largo and the mag performed flawlessly. In the next three days four buried wrecks were found. None contained treasure, yet we felt for the first time we were ready for a serious effort.

Since I was still in the process of selling stock and we were trying to keep our payroll at a minimum, I had remained in St. Louis. How- ever, every chance I had I would join them. For me things hadn't changed yet and because of that I was able to detect the subtle differ- ences in the others. It was mostly petty bickering I saw. It was a warning, but I didn't know how to handle it, or even if I was reading it correctly.

On my final visit before the beginning of the falling apart, the situation appeared to have corrected itself. Perhaps it was just because I was to find the first treasure for World Wide and to me everything looked great.

*Ships and airplanes have disappeared without a trace in an area roughly the shape of a triangle that extends into the ocean beyond Bermuda. One point of the triangle is at Miami.

The treasure came in the form of rare 1732 Pillar Dollars I had taken from conglomerate I had picked off the galleon *Infante*. The galleon was one of many of the Spanish treasure fleet that went down in the Keys during the hurricane on July 15, 1733.

The fleet had been hauling the storehouse of years of treasure, including the first coins ever milled in the New World, the 1732 Pillar Dollars. At the time I found those on the *Infante* there were few of these coins known, which made them valuable, confirming Harold's belief that I had some special kind of luck.

A 1771 Pillar Dollar found by Roy Volker in Florida waters.
(Dick Richmond Photo)

If so, I never had it there again. We worked the *Infante* many times after that and never had much to show for our efforts.

The *Infante* is at Conch Key, one of the sites thought to be the Los Mimbres of the *Maravillas*. We were searching for anything and not the *Maravillas* in particular. In spite of that, the search would have to count as my first in the pursuit of Orellana's elusive galleon. I would come back.

In the months of fruitless hunting, Art had grown quiet. He would joke like he used to, but I could tell that things were happening inside. Harold had developed a short fuse. George had become more cynical.

Roy Volker (left) with singer Bobby Rydell, whom he taught to dive in Puerto Rico.

Even when everything works properly, treasure hunting can be frustrating. A person has to contend with a lot of imponderables. Of these, the weather is the biggest. Shortly after I returned home, the weather in Florida turned nasty and the ocean became rough. One storm followed another and each time the *Virg a Lona* set out, she was driven back to shore.

Sitting on the beach, knowing each day means less money in the treasury, can cause men to grow testy. One afternoon George and Harold were feeling the cramp of being ashore and what started out as a discussion developed into a first-rate argument.

There are some people who really don't have to say anything to get under your skin. They'll make little noises or twitch or just stare. George could get to Harold by smirking, and Harold had become a screamer.

The atmosphere of verbal exchange became hot and Harold lost his cool. ''Shut your mouth,'' he warned George, ''or I'll come across this deck and shut it for you.''

George laughed. It was a dare and Harold knew it. Both men were husky and could take care of themselves, but it was to be no standoff. Harold glared at George and George let out a howl to taunt him.

Jumping to his bare feet, Harold dashed across the deck for George . . . and almost made it. Halfway there he stubbed a big toe on the motor box and fell to the deck in pain.

Ten minutes later, when George had finished laughing, he helped Harold to the car and drove him to a doctor. The toe was broken and it kept Harold from diving for three weeks.

It was the first physical sign our little group was splitting. The storm warnings were there, but none of us saw them in time.

The falling apart was not over beach madness, but over the division of responsibility. It seemed equally shared, yet every outfit needs one leader. Ours was no exception.

Art was the divemaster, and in charge of operations once a wreck was found and being worked. George was our captain and in charge of the boat while searching and en route. Harold was our magnetometer operator and in charge of all on-the-spot paperwork and of negotiations.

As I look at it now, it appears to have been a good arrangement. Those things always look good on paper because on paper all the human emotions can be ignored. Ambitions, desires, sloughing off, individual energies and idiocyncracies are never listed.

Flexibility was missing from our set-up because we saw the limitations of the others without being sure of our own. Since there was no one in absolute control of the operation, the three came into conflict at times as to who was to do what. It created problems and hard feelings. Art soon tired of the problems.

One night he telephoned me and threatened to quit unless he was placed in complete charge. ''In every company,'' he complained, ''there's one person who calls the shots. There has to be someone who makes the final decisions. That someone should be me.''

In most businesses I felt this was true, but decided it did not have to apply to treasure hunting. What did I know? I was still a treasure hunter in name only. I couldn't side with Art without alienating Harold and George. We had a real problem and while we were pondering it, Art Hartman walked away.

A week after he left the outfit, I realized he was right, and how much we needed him. Art could do anything and make everything. Fights ensued between Harold and George, and within a few months George walked away, too.

George Traber on the deck of the **Virg a Lona** *suits up for a dive on a wreck in Florida while working for World Wide Treasure Research, Inc. in 1965.*

(Roy Volker Photo)

5

INTO TREASURE HUNTING FEET FIRST —
FLAT FEATS

THINGS WERE HAPPENING OVER WHICH I SEEMED to have no control. I had been a man seeking a little adventure and the enthusiasm of the others had dragged me along. Since raising the money had been up to me, I was left with a responsibility that did not trouble the others. I had to make World Wide work if I could for our investors.

My days as a full-time family man and a sometime treasure hunter were about to reverse. What I did not realize was how radically.

I wasn't a treasure hunter; in reality I wasn't even much of a diver. My career as a boxer had ended abruptly on the head of a fighter from Puerto Rico. The blow had bent my right forefinger. Now my career as a phonograph record company executive was coming to a close because of a series of rabbit punches and I was the punchee. What was being bent out of shape this time was my life.

I suppose I was a little frightened. There's something about burning bridges behind you. It made me understand the changes in Art and Harold.

Before I was to take the big step, Harold had hired Bill Filer to replace George Traber as our boat captain. Harold telephoned me to tell me about it.

"Our operation is going again," he said. "I hired a kid . . . good diver . . . and a guy by the name of Bill Filer as captain. Roy, he seems to know everyone. More than that, he knows the Florida waters."

"Good guy?" I asked.

"We get along beautifully."

That's what I wanted to hear. I also wanted to know about the things that were happening in Florida since the big finds by Real

Eight and Treasure Salvors. Everything was not as it should have been and we were beginning to see the handwriting in the sand. We had a search lease. If we found a wreck and wanted to work it, it was necessary for us to apply for a pinpoint lease, which made good sense. That way the state could monitor the finds and keep control.

"There are some strange things happening down here," Harold reported. "There are rumors about the state closing down everyone except Real Eight and Treasure Salvors."

"They can't do that," I protested. "There are laws, and we did everything according to the state's own laws."

"It's just a rumor," Harold said.

But it wasn't just a rumor and I suppose we both sensed it. Earlier, on one of my trips south, we decided to see if the state was going to play by their own rules. We moved some timbers and ballast to a spot near an area in which we had a wreck. Then I applied for a pinpoint lease on the false site. The day after the application was made another outfit was on our newly created "wreck" blowing holes in the sand.

That told us what we needed to know. Somebody in Tallahassee was feeding the information back to a big and powerful outfit that had just moved into the Keys. A few years later Art Hartman, when he was running his own show, had problems with this same outfit trying to jump his claim. He foiled them by sprinkling small magnets throughout the area of the wreck site. When the claim jumpers tried to locate his wreck with their magnetometer, the magnets made it appear to have gone haywire. The claim jumpers had their electronics torn apart and put back together several times before they finally gave up.

And speaking of trouble with a magnetometer, we were again having problems with ours.

"It's working on a hit-and-miss basis," Harold said. "Mostly miss."

Compared to what happened next, that was just a minor irritant. Harold called again, and from the distress in his voice, I knew we were in some kind of real trouble.

"The kid has quit to go back to school," he said.

"Hire another kid."

Then he dropped the bomb. "Our lease has been cancelled," he said, quietly.

"What!" I screamed.

"All leases have been cancelled until new regulations can be written into Florida laws regarding treasure hunting."

"Any exceptions?" I wanted to know.

"Real Eight and Treasure Salvors."

When I hung up the phone, I knew that Harold was probably feeling as bad as I. The blow was a serious one because we had no way of knowing how long it would take before the new regulations would be in force. Nor did we have any assurance that once they were in force that we would be granted a new lease.

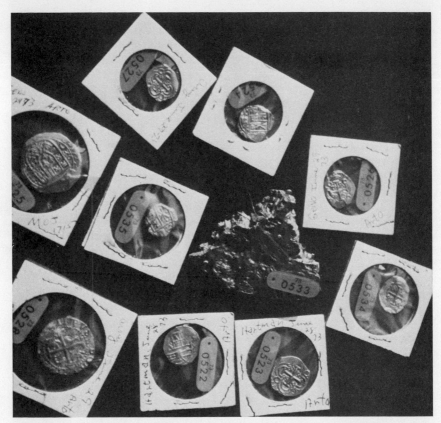

A gold wedge and gold coins brought up from the bones of the 1715 fleet by the crew of Doubloon Salvage. The numbers are those made by the Florida state representative so as to catalog the treasure recovered.   *(Art Hartman Photo)*

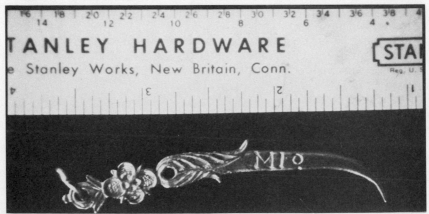

A gold toothpick found on the 1715 wrecks.   *(Art Hartman Photo)*

Until the big finds on the 1715 fleet, the State of Florida paid little attention to the offshore wrecks. Those things that were being brought up from the ocean and preserved were done so by men who had risked their capital, their time, and often their lives to recover things that had lain on the bottom of the ocean for hundreds of years. They had learned how to preserve their finds because it was profitable to do so. It was free enterprise at its best.

No one was concerned about preserving archeological sites until there was treasure involved. Not that anyone could see those archeological sites even if they were left untampered. Most often they were buried under sand and coral in areas where, even if uncovered, the sea would bury them again. That which was buried was, for the most part, nothing but rubble.

In the free enterprise system, the state was taking precautions to guard its share, which in Florida is twenty-five per cent. In this way the state benefits because private money and not public money is going into obtaining and preserving the treasure. The public benefits, too, because items of history that may otherwise have been lost forever are now available to see.

Then, too, the state has an opportunity to weigh the finds carefully. Everything belongs to the state until a division of the treasure is made. When it is made, and this is usually after a period of one year, the state has first choice of the finds.

Furthermore, bonding is required and those bonds run into thousands of dollars. Any violation of the regulations would result in a treasure-hunting company having to forfeit its bond and lose its lease. That in itself would keep a company cautious. Too much in time, equipment and money is at stake to take a chance on violating the regulations.

We could understand the state being cautious about handing out leases on a wholesale basis. A man from the newly formed Florida Department of Antiquities had to be present when an outfit was working a wreck. Those who were qualified for this kind of work were limited in number, and their being present was an additional expense.

Yet we had the boat, equipment, financial backing and by then, the trained personnel to do the job. We had also followed all the regulations and bonding procedures required by the state. However, we were without a lease.

Still we were not dead. Now was the time for me to make a move. Harold had been asking me for months to come to Florida and help with the operation. I discussed the situation with several of World Wide's financial backers, who agreed that I should be there. With that I resigned from my job.

We needed a fourth man, one who was both a diver and a mechanic. I remembered Dave Meinell, who was about to be discharged from the Army. Dave agreed to join us.

Three days after he arrived in St. Louis from Germany, we left for Florida. We had lost our lease, but at the time in the Keys trea-

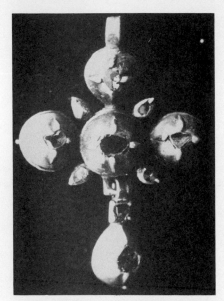

A silver cross with rough diamonds from an unidentified French wreck in Florida Keys.
(Dick Richmond Photo)

sure hunters were permitted to work outside the three-mile limit. That would change, too, after Tom Gurr found the 1733 galleon, *San Jose*, more than four miles offshore of Monroe County.

The State of Florida then decided its territorial waters did not stop at the traditional three-mile distance from shore. The ruling was in the Keys the territorial limit extended to three miles beyond the Florida Reef or into the Gulf Stream, whichever was further.

What it amounted to was that the only coast state in the United States to extend its territorial limits to twelve miles was Florida, and even that was done on a selective basis — to the area where the wrecks were. Since the *San Jose* was in that area, Gurr was ordered to stop digging. In 1975 the United States Supreme Court ruled against Florida regarding the extension of its territorial waters.

Dave and I drove straight through to Key Largo, arriving the next day just in time to join Harold and Bill Filer as they were about to set sail to check out a wreck they had found the afternoon before. It was in 160 feet of water.

Dave had never before been on a boat the size of the *Virg a Lona* and he spent the better part of an hour inspecting the engine room, living quarters and storage compartments. He loved it, but his opinion regarding her seaworthiness would change radically before we finally had to leave Florida for the West Indies.

When we set sail, I could feel Bill Filer taking the measure of Dave and me. Bill was shorter than the rest of us, stockily built and with one of those whispering laughs that seem low but can be heard everywhere. I discovered he wasn't quick to judge, and when he did size up a man, he accepted him for what he was. Harold was right about Bill being an excellent seaman. What was more, he was an excellent, even-tempered man who never seemed to become angry or out of sorts about anything.

Anchoring over the wreck area, Harold suited up to dive and to take a look. When he and Bill had found the wreck the day before, the mag had gone wild. However, it had been too late in the day for them to check it out.

As Harold was putting on his gear, Dave put on his. "You ever make a 160-foot dive before, Dave?'' Harold asked. He knew he had not because the only time Dave had ever been diving was when he went to the lakes with us. Dave was a novice, who, in a year's time, would develop into one of the best divers I have ever seen. When we arrived in Florida, the best he could do on a free dive was thirty feet. In a few months he would be making free dives of 100 feet regularly. He was grace underwater. On top of the water was something else again. You will be learning a lot about Dave in the next several chapters.

Dave grinned at Harold's question. ''Nope,'' he replied, ''but if I'm going to do this for a living, I may as well start now.''

Harold did not look too confident. ''OK,'' he said, ''but don't wander off down there.''

The dive only lasted five minutes. No sooner had they reached the bottom than they found a World War II Liberty ship with a huge hole in the middle of her water line. Apparently she had been torpedoed by a German submarine in the early days of the war.

As Harold was slipping off his tank, he whispered to me about Dave, ''That kid is really cool under water.''

Two days later Dave had his first test against sharks. It was late in the afternoon and Harold detected what he hoped would be a wreck. Each time we passed over the spot where he was getting a hit, we threw a buoy. After five passes, we had a cluster of buoys. It was worth a look.

Dave volunteered to check it out and flipped over the side. Snorkeling over the spot where we had dropped the buoys, he made an exploratory dive to inspect the bottom.

When he popped to the surface, he yelled, ''I can't see anything. It must be buried under the sand.'' He was about 400 feet away.

''OK,'' I called, and waved him back to the boat.

About halfway back I heard him let out a yelp, then saw him swimming as fast as I've ever seen any man travel in water under his own power. He was yelling as he came.

Harold, who was at the wheel, spun the boat around to close the gap. The engines probably frightened away the five sharks that had given Dave such a scare. They were nowhere to be seen when he climbed aboard.

Bill Filer, who had joined me at the stern to help pull Dave out of the water, yelled, ''Don't bring those damn things with you!'' Then laughed.

However, neither the sharks nor the comment were funny to Dave. He was quiet for the next few hours. The incident apparently did something to him because after that a shark was not safe in the same water with him. If he saw a shark, he went after it with spear and bangstick.*

Because our magnetometer was so important to us we had to have someone upon whom we could rely to repair it. John Kowalski, a

*A bangstick is a pole with an explosive device at its tip.

Dave Meinell with a pesky shark he shot in the Caymans.
(Roy Volker Photo)

neighbor in St. Louis, and I had become friends. John wanted to be part of our operation. All we really needed was an electronics expert. I didn't think John fit that category.

Wrong! That's what I was. John was not trained in electronics, but he taught himself what made a magnetometer tick, and eventually developed his own model. He also built sensing heads for the mag and the first metal detector I was to use.

However, that was later. When I first arrived in Florida to permanently join the outfit on a full-time basis, our mag was undependable. We were never able to use it more than one day in a row.

The *Maravillas* came up more and more in our conversations. Poring over the research night after night, Harold and I decided to check out Conch Key once more. Conch Key is a squat little island on which sits some squat houses on stilts. Without the houses, the key is a desolate unfriendly place, and it didn't take much to guess what it was like in 1656 as a shipwrecked sailor. The one thing that troubled me about searching at Conch Key was that even a mile or two out we were still too close to land.

Very few of the 700 aboard Orellana's galleon had survived. It did not seem a logical place. Yet we searched, and searched. We were finding nothing that we did not already know was there. Still, we were becoming organized treasure hunters, learning how to grid an area so that we weren't just wandering about the ocean in a random pattern.

We were confining our activities to the water beyond the three-mile territorial limit. After weeks of looking, we knew we were wasting our time. The *Maravillas* had to be in one of the three places referred to as Los Mimbres in the Bahamas.

Harold and I flew to Nassau to discuss with government officials there the possibilities of obtaining a search lease. They were not interested in handing out leases to us or to anyone else. Treasure hunters who could no longer legally search the offshore waters of Florida were sneaking into Bahamian waters working wrecks without permission. The government did not want to have anything to do with any of us.

A bell and cross found by Roy Volker on a wreck near Conch Key, Florida.
(Dick Richmond Photo)

On the return flight from Nassau we felt defeated. We were quiet, but I had come to the conclusion if we were to continue treasure hunting, it would have to be away from the States. Harold agreed but had nothing to suggest. We had heard South America was almost untouched by treasure hunters. However, we had also heard North Americans just did not go there and start digging. Without someone there pulling strings for you, a person could easily wind up in jail.

There were other things that made us look somewhere other than South America. None of us spoke Spanish. We would need the *Virg a Lona* and I had my doubts the boat was capable of making such a voyage. Even if she did make it, repairs there might be impossible because parts would not be available. Most importantly, we would be searching in remote areas, and if the mag broke down completely, we would be out of business.

Cuba and Cuba's Isle of Pines would be ideal — out of the question for Americans. We were stymied. So we continued to work beyond the three-mile limit. The thought of moving our operation was never long out of our conversations.

A jade figure taken off a wreck in the Florida Keys in 1965.
(Dick Richmond Photo)

Harold and I returned to the research he had brought back from Spain. As others had done before and since, he had learned of the twenty-eight-ship plate fleet that had been hit by a violent hurricane on September 6, 1622.

Pieces of eight found in Florida by Volker in 1965.
(Dick Richmond Photo)

Among the nine ships that sank were the galleons *Margarita* and *Nuestra Senora de Atocha*. Both had been loaded with treasure when they went down, and nothing from the *Atocha*, the almiranta of the fleet, had ever been salvaged.

We really had very little on which to base a search, except a general location, and the report that the *Atocha* was supposed to have been carrying about $2,000,000 in gold and silver and the *Margarita* about $1,500,000 when they went down. We also knew the storm had torn the galleons apart so we were not likely to find the wrecks and their treasures in a nice convenient lump. In spite of that we felt it was worth a try. What did we have to lose; there was nowhere else to go. So we moved our operation south for about a month. It was like searching an underwater desert.

At Christmas, I flew to St. Louis to be with my family. It was at a party there that everything turned around again. I was discussing our problem with a group of friends and one of the group mentioned the Caymans, three small islands south of Cuba in the British West Indies. He said he did not know if treasure had ever been found there; however, the islands were littered with wrecks.

When I returned to Florida, Harold and I took a plane to Grand Cayman. We looked the situation over and discussed a lease arrangement with the islands' administrator, the Honorable John Cumber.

Cumber called a meeting of Grand Cayman's five-man governing board of elected islanders, at which we were allowed to explain our proposition. We told them who we were and what we wanted to do. A lease was drawn and we agreed on a division if we found anything.

The Caymans would receive twenty-five per cent. It was an exclusive lease in a virgin territory loaded with wrecks. For the first time since we had started on this venture we had something to cheer about. Still, there are no calm seas in treasure hunting.

Harold was once again his old self, bursting with enthusiasm, filled wth good humor and ready for anything. Almost anything. No one was prepared for what happened next.

After we arrived back in Key Largo, the next week was spent in hauling the *Virg a Lona*. Harold spent part of the time in Miami with his family. He had a wife, Betty, two daughters and a young son. The son was having some problems with illness, and he was always a concern to Harold.

After a week we were ready to go. We planned to run from Key

Largo to Key West, where we would top off our fuel before heading for Cuba to make the turn around San Antonio Light at the western tip of the island. There we would set a new course for Grand Cayman.

Just before we were to leave, Harold suggested I fly over to pick up copies of our lease agreement. That way I could spend a few days getting acquainted and could chat with some of the fishermen to check if any of them had ever come upon a deep-water ballast pile.

Docking had to be arranged. Also I had to check on where we would get our best buy on fuel and supplies. It was a logical suggestion and I agreed.

Harold was to send me a cable when the *Virg a Lona* was to depart from Key West.

Arriving in Grand Cayman the next day, I immediately picked up our lease agreements and then accomplished the other chores. The rest of the day and part of the night were spent talking to fishermen about wrecks. These men had spent the greater part of their lives looking for fish through glass-bottom buckets. If anyone knew where deep wrecks were, they would. I offered cash to anyone who could show me a ballast pile in deep water; I even went so far as to run an advertisement in the Cayman newspaper. No takers.

The cable arrived; the *Virg a Lona* had left Key West. I still had things to do. Knowing we would need some sort of transportation, I shopped for a car. We did not have much money and anything that would run was tagged with a price way beyond what we could pay. Finally I found a '51 Chevrolet that had four wheels that rolled and a motor that functioned, occasionally at the same time. Dave Meinell could make anything run, although this was to be a challenge to him.

The day the *Virg a Lona* was to arrive came and passed. Becoming worried, I went to the only long-range radio shack on the island. Between calls of regular traffic, the radio operator tried to reach the *Virg a Lona.* Nothing.

The next day we tried again, but received no response. When the *Virg a Lona* was thirty-six hours overdue, I knew my friends were in trouble. Finally, Grand Cayman radio broke through to the United States Coast Guard at Key West. The word we received was that the *Virg a Lona* and her crew were on a reef inside Cuban waters off Santa Lucia Light. There was no further information available at that time.

I was sick. This had to be big trouble, considering that relations between the United States and Cuba were at an extreme low. It was two days before I was able to obtain more news. I was advised the *Virg a Lona* and her crew were being held by Cuban immigration for illegal entry into the country.

We had guns and dynamite aboard and all I could think of was the Bay of Pigs. Returning to Florida, I checked with the government agency in contact with the Swiss Embassy in Cuba. The Swiss were representing United States interests there.

I was advised to keep quiet and to stay away from reporters.

Everything possible was being done that could be done. However, if the news of the *Virg a Lona* and her crew leaked out to the press, it might make it harder to arrange for the release of my friends.

I had no choice. I sat and waited.

Since the incident happened to Dave Meinell, I'll let him relate it.

(From left): Dave Meinell, Harold Still and Jack McBeth pictured as Still and Meinell left for Grand Cayman after the Cuban Jail Affair.   *(Roy Volker Photo)*

Harold Still on the stern of the Virg a Lona *as the boat was being prepared for the voyage to Grand Cayman Island.* *(Roy Volker Photo)*

6

THE CUBAN JAIL AFFAIR
By Dave Meinell

█ WAS IN THE ARMY STATIONED IN GERMANY when I received
a letter from my long-time friend, Roy Volker, telling me that he
had a place for me in his treasure-hunting outfit. I was a diver, a
mechanic and a demolitions man. He said he needed me. It was
June, 1965. At twenty-five years of age, it was like a dream come
true.

If I had known then that in a few months the dream would turn into
a nightmare — that I would be sitting in a jail cell in Havana,
Cuba — I'm not sure I would have been all that ready to sign on. But
no one knows those things and three days after my discharge from
the Army I was on my way to Florida ready to become an adventurer.

The adventure was there all right, but mostly treasure hunting
turned out to be hard work with water in the ears. Yet that didn't
matter; I was doing something that most men can only imagine.

I had been with World Wide about three months when it was decided to move the operation to Grand Cayman Island, which is south
of Cuba. That suited me fine. Florida waters are murky compared
to those in the Caribbean. If we were going to pick on wrecks, it
would be nice to see what we were doing for a change instead of
working in the dark.

Bill Filer, Harold Still and I were to take the *Virg a Lona* to Cayman. Roy was to fly over and meet us there.

Sailing out of Key Largo, we moved south to Key West. At Key
West, Bill and I chatted with several shrimp fishermen about the
journey around Cuba. They told us about the light at Santa Lucia and
the one at San Antonio, which is at the westernmost tip of Cuba. We
were warned that if we made our turn too soon going around the tip,
we would wind up in the Great Sound and probably hit a reef.

Nodding our heads as if we had good sense, we left the shrimpers certain that we could miss an island as large as Cuba if we wanted to.

It was November and the seas were calm as long as we stayed in the channel between Key West and Cuba. It was like running on the Mississippi River. The only difference was the ground swells.

As soon as we spotted Cuba, we ran west parallel to it, keeping about twelve miles out. The *Virg a Lona,* even with its twin diesels, was only capable of about thirteen knots. So we were about thirty-five hours out of Key West when the discussion began as to whether we had reached the point to make our turn and head south.

Actually the discussion was between Harold and Bill. I was there, but I wasn't asked for my opinion. Not that I had one. At any rate, after forty-five minutes of talking about it, we made the turn.

It was about 3:30 in the afternoon and the sun on the water was a glare. It was pretty, but it was like driving into a fire. We were sailing blind.

We never saw the reef until after we hit it. Luckily the *Virg a Lona* only drew thirty-eight inches of water. The reef was just under the surface, perhaps thirty to thirty-five inches. If it had been closer to the top, we might have knocked a hole in the bow or run aground.

As soon as we hit, Bill shut off the engines and we drifted over the top into water about seventy feet deep. Immediately I donned my diving gear and went over the side. The starboard propeller and shaft were bent and there was a chunk out of the port prop.

Even damaged the port prop was in good enough shape to get us out. That's when we discoverd that there was something wrong with the port engine. We were not to discover exactly what until nearly a month later.

There was no immediate danger of sinking. We were just stuck. Since we didn't know what do do next, we made the only decision open to us: we decided to spend the night.

At sunrise I was down in the hold to check the damage and discovered the port engine was full of water. That meant that the good engine had the bad shaft and prop and the engine filled with water had the serviceable shaft and prop. It was a lousy combination, but I thought I could do something about it. What I didn't know was that the water in the engine was coming in through the exchanger in a bad bushing in the water pump.

I drained the water and the oil out of the engine. There were two leaks and I repaired them. With that accomplished, we refilled the engine. As soon as we put water into it, it flowed right into the crankcase.

By now we knew we were in Cuban waters, but we were totally immobile. There was nothing to do but call for help. So Harold radioed the United States Coast Guard at Key West.

During the night that we had spent sitting there, we had seen the light at Santa Lucia. Timing it, we had a pretty good idea of where we were. We had made exactly the mistake the shrimpers had warned us against. They had told us to stay in the main shipping lanes until we were sure. We had turned too soon.

After Harold explained our situation to the Coast Guard and reported our position, we were told to stand by until contacted. It was afternoon before they got back to us and said that someone had been notified to come to our aid. It turned out to be Cuban marines.

Every man has his own fears. I didn't know mine until I saw those two Russian-made Cuban torpedo boats bearing down on us loaded to the rails with thirty to forty men armed with automatic weapons. If they were coming to our aid, they sure didn't look too happy about it.

Pulling alongside, several of the men jumped onto the *Virg a Lona* and started shouting at us. I didn't understand the words, but I sure understood the gestures. Those big guns said to me, "Dave, climb aboard that torpedo boat." Then the guns pointed Harold, Bill and me forward where we were led to a hatch. We were directed to climb below into a rope locker.

The rope locker was four feet high by about five wide and eight long. But it was far from empty. I'm six-foot-three and there didn't seem to be enough room in there even for me. Yet the guns didn't seem in any mood for hesitation and in I went. Harold, who is six feet tall, followed me. Bill, all five-foot-ten of him, joined us. Bill was no sooner down than the hatch cover closed over the top of us, leaving us in complete and extremely crowded blackness.

There is no way to describe how scared I was, except to say it got worse once the boat got under way. We were right in the bow next to the skin of the prow. The boat was a metal-hulled vessel, but the Cubans were taking it across those dangerous waters at about twenty-five knots. Metal hull or not, we knew if that boat hit a reef at the speed we were traveling, the bottom would be ripped out and that would be it for three would-be treasure finders who happened to turn left too soon. I kept thinking, If I ever get out of this alive . . . If I ever get out of this alive . . .

We were picked up about the same time of the afternoon in which we had run onto the reef the day before. For the most part we were quiet while in the rope locker, but Bill mentioned in passing that he hoped the Cubans knew the channel. They didn't.

It seemed as if we had been in darkness for hours when the torpedo boat hit the reef. There was a terrible crunch and we went flying against one another. We expected water to come rushing in, but it didn't. When we finally untangled ourselves from one another, we realized we weren't moving.

"We've run aground," Bill remarked.

A minute later the hatch cover was thrown back and sunlight flooded in. I remember being surprised it was still daylight. However, I didn't have time to ponder it. The big guns were urging us to climb out and move back to the stern.

We were high and dry. If we had hit the reef at high tide, we were going to be higher and dryer before the night was over. The way the boat was sitting, I knew if the water level dropped two feet, we would capsize and go tumbling into the sea.

Not long after we hit, the boat towing the *Virg a Lona* pulled up and anchored nearby. So even if the boat which we were on did roll over, we would probably reach safety. However, the guns, which were now starting to acquire faces, seemed to regard their folly as our fault. We could feel the hostility growing.

Three big men trying to make themselves smaller is no easy task, yet we did the best we could. We sat quietly without moving.

One of the officers spoke a little English. It was he who handed us safety jackets and told us not to worry. We were aground, he said, but help was on its way.

By dark we were still on the reef. The ground swells started and they would lift the vessel and bounce it hard against the reef, making the whole thing quiver. The current was runing and now we weren't sure we could make it to the other boats if we happened to capsize.

However, as our situation seemed to get worse regarding the state of the vessel, our position with the crew was improving. Two of the guards were only boys, perhaps sixteen. They were dressed in just swimming trunks and as evening became night and the wind and water whipped over us, they grew cold. To keep them warm we had them huddle with us.

Sometime during the night the tide rose enough for us to float free. When we did, the three of us cheered as loudly as the Cubans. From that moment on we were no longer treated as hostiles but as unfortunate seamen.

That, however, improved my own mental attitude only slightly. I didn't say so, but I was still concerned, largely because of the uncertainty of what might happen when we reached shore. What did happen seems strange in retrospect. At the time it was downright weird.

Santa Lucia is a poor little place with grass huts and dirt streets. Everyone was out for our arrival, staring at us as we were taken to an old barracks. There we were questioned separately by high-ranking officers.

My interrogator was very courteous. He was middle-aged, well-groomed, soft-spoken. Everyone wore the same fatigue uniform so the only way to tell rank was by insignia. There was nothing in his actions that would have made me uneasy; it was his line of questioning. For the first time I realized we might be in even more trouble than I thought initially, and my first thought was we were in up to our necks.

In the excitement of everything that had been happening, none of us — Harold, Bill nor I — had thought our equipment might be considered incriminating. We were carrying a high-powered rifle, dynamite, plastic explosives and the other paraphernalia for working a wreck.

I explained to him that whenever there were divers in the water, there was always someone aboard with a rifle in case of sharks. The explosives were there because anytime something sinks in tropical waters, it is quickly encrusted in coral. Frequently, small charges were used to break something loose.

The main issue regarding the questioning centered around the possibility of our being connected with some counter-revolutionary outfit. The interrogator wanted to know whether we knew anyone in Cuba and just how much knowledge we had of the land and the off-shore waters. I think it became apparent to him that if we knew any-thing about the offshore waters, we wouldn't be in the fix we were in.

I explained to him I was from the Midwest and had never seen the ocean until three months prior to our arrest. He was curious then as to why I would travel 1500 miles to Florida just to go off on an ad-venture. I told him my reasons, which I had begun to question myself.

Sometime during the day a large Russian-made helicopter flew in to pick up a half dozen of the Cubans and us. We were being moved to the province capital, Pinar del Rio, for further questioning . . . and a party.

Our arrival had given excuse for a number of leaders in this moun-tainous area who had fought with Fidel Castro to have their first reunion since the revolution.

When the helicopter set down at Pinar del Rio, we were picked up by a dilapidated 1956 Oldsmobile, which I later discovered was held together by coat hangers, bubble gum and a great deal of ingenuity. The Oldsmobile delivered us to an old stone building on a narrow street where we were taken to the second floor.

There were perhaps forty people there. Two large tables were filled with food. As soon as we walked in, the Cubans who had arrived with us and those already there started shaking hands and clapping one another on the back. There was nothing else for us to do but stand there like three large lumps.

That didn't last long. After a short period of private questioning in another room by a white-haired officer of about sixty, who iden-tified himself as an official in the Castro regime, we were asked to rejoin the party. We were introduced to everyone in an air of com-plete cordiality. With so many, it was like emptying a bag of marbles onto the floor and then saying pick one out. Besides, all I could see was the food table. It had been twenty hours or more since we had last eaten. The three of us must have looked like vultures.

That party was just the first in a week of good times for the crew of the *Virg a Lona*. At this time we had no idea of where the boat was. We were not to see her again until the day we left.

After the party we were driven in the Oldsmobile from Pinar del Rio to Havana. It was late by the time we arrived and we were taken to the Marine headquarters building, an old stone affair on the harbor. There was a balcony in our room, which up to the time of our arrival had belonged to two junior officers. From the balcony we could watch the vessels moving in and out of the harbor.

During the day, we had an area in which we could move about

freely. The interpreter who had been assigned to us pointed to a door and told us we were not to go through there. On the other side of the door was a soldier with a grease gun. As far as we were concerned, the grease gun was explanation enough as to why we should not trespass. When we were told that, I was sure there was nothing I wanted to do on the other side of that door. But I forgot and almost didn't live to regret it.

In the daytime for us it was the Marine headquarters building; at night it was party time. The interpreter took us out in the evening, chauffeured in that rattly Olds, to the best places in Havana. We only had the clothes we were wearing when taken prisoner. I was dressed in black wash-and-wear slacks, a white T-shirt and white tennis shoes. Bill and Harold didn't look much better.

There we were rubbing elbows with the beautiful people in gowns and tuxedos. What was neat was that even dressed as we were, we were accepted. People stared occasionally but not enough to make us uncomfortable. We figured we were being shown the glitter side of Havana to prove Cuba under Castro was not as bad as we had been led to believe.

It was all about to come to an abrupt end, but not before I came close to getting my head blown off. The atmosphere of hospitality had made us all pretty loose. I had made friends with our driver. When he kept having trouble with the automobile's generator light, I, being a mechanic, asked to take a look. It didn't take long for me to diagnose the problem and tell him what was needed.

He was sure he could not find the part; parts for American automobiles just were not available. However, he did locate what he needed in a junk yard. As soon as he discovered it, he drove to where we were staying. I was on the balcony when he arrived. He waved to me from the street, shouting he had obtained what he needed to repair the generator.

Passing through the forbidden door, I rushed down the steps. When I neared the bottom, I heard the click of the grease gun as it was cocked, then the sounds of a commotion. I stopped, took a breath, then slowly walked to the car. Later our interpreter told me the guard was new and I had come as close to taking my last deep dive as I'd ever want to.

That tightened us up a little. We again realized we were uninvited guests of the Cubans. However, the honeymoon was about over anyway. Bill and I were having a splendid time, but Harold was worried about his wife and son. The boy had been ill and Harold was sure by then his wife would know he was missing at sea or taken prisoner by the Cubans. He wanted to send word that he was all right.

He told our interpreter what he wanted to do. Our interpreter didn't come out and say so, but he hinted we should let things ride as they were. Bill and I were willing, but then we had no responsibilities other than to ourselves. Harold was insistent and we had to go along with him.

Our interpreter left and when he returned, there were two armed men with him. They took us to immigration detention. If we were interned in an immigration facility, I never want to relax in a Cuban jail.

The stone building was in the wharf section and around it was a Spanish-styled iron fence about eight feet high. Inside it was dank and about as pleasant as a bat cave. The fears that had been melting away in the last week returned with a vengeance and Bill and I blamed Harold for our situation.

Harold had been right in wanting to contact his wife, of course, but all Bill and I could think about was instead of being on an unexpected holiday, we were in jail. Besides, we had been warned to cool it. As it turned out, word was never sent to Harold's wife, but he couldn't have known. After the initial arguments, we took comfort in the fact the three of us were still together.

Inside the immigration detention building we were taken into a room surrounded by bars. Behind a wooden desk sat a short squatty man with brooding eyes and an unshaven face. Nearby sat a sleepy looking guard holding a grease gun.

As the man behind the desk took down the particulars on us, the guard didn't move, didn't blink, didn't look in our direction. The only thing that seemed to make him stir was when someone meandered too near a large white line painted on the floor about three feet in front of the desk. We were told we were to stay on the other side of the white line. After the previous incident, I was going to remember that.

As soon as the man behind the desk took the information he needed, we were marched to a cell and locked up for the night. In the daytime we were allowed to roam in the same general areas as the ten or twelve other detainees in the building. However, each evening shortly after dinner we were ordered back to our cell and locked up — for our protection, we were told.

Our bill of fare changed abruptly, too. Instead of ordering a la carte from the menu of a fancy restaurant, we were given sandwiches with mystery meat in the morning and unhulled rice and fish for lunch and dinner. I was all right in all departments until one night squid was served on top of the rice and I found mine looking at me.

When we entered the jail, there began for me and the rest two of the most dreary, uncomfortable weeks of our lives. We weren't mistreated, but no one would tell us anything. The uncertainties of what was going to happen began to gnaw at me. Confinement was making me introspective, uncommunicative.

A few days after our internment, I found a new friend, a mouse who came and joined me at mealtime. Out of a hardroll and a string, I fashioned a swing for him and as we ate, he would sit on the hard-roll and swing.

The friendship only lasted about three days. It ended suddenly one night when I forgot to feed him. I was lying on the top bunk in the cell when I heard something rattling about in our utensils. Jumping down to look, I found my mouse, who apparently was there looking for his evening handout. Coming upon him so suddenly startled him; he jumped from the ridge of stone on which the utensils were sitting and landed on Harold's naked chest. Harold leaped straight up and the mouse took off down Harold's stomach, making his getaway through Harold's skivvies.

Bill and I laughed until we thought our sides would split, but Harold didn't think it was funny. The mouse never returned. I guess the noise Harold made when the mouse landed on his chest frightened him into looking for his food elsewhere.

After about two weeks, a secretary from the Swiss Consulate arrived. He listened quietly as we painstakingly told him the entire story, then abruptly departed. The next day he returned with the Swiss Ambassador's attache'and we were set free.

When we walked out, the sleepy guard was there watching his white line. He looked up as we passed by, and I could feel him staring at our backs. It gave me the same sensation as when I found the squid on top of the rice.

From the harbor area, we were taken into an exclusive section of Havana to what had been the official residence of the United States Ambassador. After weeks of confinement, it was like a fairyland to me. There were formal gardens, stately statues and an immense swimming pool.

For the next two days that was our home. Then we were notified the *Virg a Lona* had been repaired. The shipfitters were able to replace the props and the disabled shaft on the boat, but this still left us with the engine that kept filling with water. However, the distance from Havana to Key West is only about ninety miles so we didn't think we would have any problems. There was a bill for $3700 for the repair work, which was paid before we left.

The Cuban officials who drove us to the dock returned to us everything that had been confiscated when we were taken prisoner. The items missing on the *Virg a Lona* were food, clothing and nearly everything that hadn't been nailed down. We guessed the boat been stripped by the people in Santa Lucia, who were very poor.

At the time we didn't care. All we knew was we would soon be heading back for the States. It was a good feeling.

Our troubles were far from over. A storm was brewing and our Cuban escorts tried to warn us. They were showing positive concern regarding an attempt by us to make a crossing with the weather changing the way it was.

However, we could smell freedom. The sun was still bright when we sailed out of Havana harbor. How bad could it be? Four hours out we discovered how accurate the warning had been.

The wind whipped up and the waves started to mount until they were reaching eight feet. A hundred-pound anchor forward had not been secured and with each great swell it would fly into the air and come crashing down against the bulkhead.

We knew if it wasn't secured, it would eventually crash through the hull. It had to be tied; Harold and I crawled out over the superstructure straining with every muscle to keep from being tossed into the sea. I rapped my chin hard and put a bruise the size of an orange on my right elbow before we reached the anchor. We had it secured in ten minutes, yet it seemed like hours, and when we finally made it back to the cabin, we collapsed in exhaustion.

Throughout the trip we were in constant contact with the Coast Guard. Obviously there were several Coast Guard vessels out and we were flattered to think that they were at sea during this blow just for our safety.

What we didn't know was that the same morning we left Havana, Castro had signed an agreement to allow refugees to be flown out of Cuba to the United States. About one hundred small boats waiting to carry the refugees out had been tied up at a small harbor town on the north coast of Cuba. Castro had ordered the craft out of the harbor because they were causing a health hazard. So we were just one of the scores of vessels crossing the Straits that day. We didn't know a thing about it until we reached Key West. So much for VIP treatment.

VIP's indeed! When we reached Florida, we were taken into custody again. The United States Coast Guard was there to greet us. The only difference this time was they didn't have their guns drawn and they spoke English. Again we were separated and interrogated. It was the same scene all over again only without the mouse and the sleepy Cuban guarding his white line.

Roy Volker will pick up the narrative once more.

7

ILL WIND FOR WORLD WIDE

WHEN DAVE, HAROLD AND BILL ARRIVED back at Key West, I was there to meet them. They looked like refugees, but I was never so happy to see three guys in my life. They were thinner, otherwise they were physically all right.

The *Virg a Lona* was a mess but we managed to run it up to Key Largo, where we had it hauled out of the water to be refitted with new shafts and props. The port engine was also repaired.

As soon as Harold was able, he took off for Miami to see his family. Dave and Bill, however, stuck around long enough to help me get the boat off the drydock run. With that done, they disappeared, too.

It was a week before I saw Dave and Bill again and three days more before Harold made an appearance. His son was fine. The first night after everyone was gone I went to sleep concerned about the problems with which we were faced, with which *I* was faced.

No sooner had I arrived in Florida than Harold handed over the reins of the company to me. Nothing was said; the transfer of command so to speak was implicit. I guess he felt he had had a shot and had accomplished nothing of any value. It would be up to me.

Being with Harold when he was on his feed was neat. His personality made him the best kind of companion, sometimes nutty, sometimes philosophical, most of the time enthusiastic, always in there doing his share or more. But Harold wasn't on his feed.

After Cuba his fuse was so short that for the first time he and I got into arguments, mostly because I didn't respond to his *orders* as quickly as he thought I should, and he would scream at me.

We were in Grand Cayman working when we almost came to blows.

52

Something wasn't as Harold thought it should be and he let me have it at the top of his lungs.

"Don't scream at me, you S.O.B.," I warned.

With that Harold whirled around and came at me, fists clenched.

"Harold," I said softly. "I know you want to hit me, but if you do, I'll beat your brains out."

He stopped in his tracks, turned on his heel and went into the cabin. Harold could take care of himself, and I was well aware that if I had taken a swing, I would have known I was in a fight.

Yet we had not come to that point. We were still on the beach in Florida. Our boat was functional but in general disrepair. Harold worried me and Bill gave me no kind of reassurance. At that moment I wasn't certain if we had finally come to an end as a company or if we would make another attempt to salvage something out of all the troubles we seemed to be having.

The next morning I started in on the work that had to be done. I did not know what I was hoping to accomplish, but I had been sitting for weeks and I had to do something. I guess what I was really thinking was if I put the *Virg a Lona* shipshape once more, my three companions would not mind making another attempt.

For days I cleaned, scraped and painted. I scrubbed the bilges, aired the mattresses, lubricated every compressor, motor and engine aboard. Both engines were turned over daily until they began to sound right. More importantly, the boat began to look right.

By the time the crew returned, the *Virg a Lona* sparkled. Everyone was impressed, including Bill Filer. However, Bill was through with treasure hunting. Harold was under a strain and looked it. His wife had thought he had been killed and was against him continuing. In spite of that Harold decided to make another try with us. Dave was ready for anything.

Our trip to Grand Cayman was uneventful. This time we made sure there was at least thirty miles between us and Cuba.

Our first day on the island was spent basically doing household chores. The next day we started to work the first of more than forty wrecks we would find in the year we were there.

By this time Mel Fisher had introduced the propwash blower system into treasure hunting and we had ours. Airlifts, basically the only tools available for digging in deep water (more than forty feet), are like toys compared to the blowers.

The blowers are simple devices really. When a wreck is found, mailbox affairs are placed over the propellers. Then two stern anchors are set and one bow anchor. When the engines are revved, the thrust of the propellers is forced downward and the pressure of the water removes the sand from a wreck in minutes instead of days and weeks, which is often the case when airlifts have to be employed.

Our first wreck produced a number of nice artifacts but no treasure. It was, however, a start. And, every day from 7 in the morning until dusk we worked. We weren't bothering anyone or so we thought. As usual, we were wrong. One night the British adminis-

Spanish crosses taken off wrecks in the Cayman Islands by Roy Volker.

(Dick Richmond Photo)

trator, John Cumber, who was to become a good friend, mentioned one of the islanders was complaining to him about us. The islander ran a charter business and was afraid we were there to move in on him.

"His name is Bob Soto," John told me. "He has a sixty-foot, single-diesel boat called the *Cayman Pilot*, and charters it for diving and fishing trips."

Early the next morning I went to see Bob at his dive shop. He is a large, muscular man of about six feet. When I told him who I was, he regarded me cautiously with his dark eyes. I had discovered from John that Bob's air compressor, which he used to fill scuba tanks, wasn't functioning. So I had ours taken off the boat and brought up to his shop.

"Look!" I told him, "we'll be operating off a large airbank on the *Virg a Lona*. We'll just keep this here and you can use it while you're getting yours repaired. I'll have one of my mates, Dave Meinell, take a look at yours to see if he can fix it."

Then we discussed fuel and supplies and the other things we would be needing while there. Before I left I had Bob convinced we

A bell on a semi-modern wreck found by Roy Volker and company in the Cayman Islands.

(Roy Volker Photo)

An old fisherman and his dog sail out to the Virg a Lona *in the Caymans to show Volker a wreck he had spotted.*   (Roy Volker Photo)

had not come to Grand Cayman to move in on his charter business, only to treasure hunt. When that was clearly understood, his attitude changed completely.

I was to learn later Bob Soto's wife and Art McKee's wife are sisters. The two men not only knew each other but had worked wrecks together, including the galleon *Genovesa*, which sank on Pedro Bank in 1730. Bob and I were one day to make an attempt to salvage the rich wreck, but that's told in a later chapter.

Week followed week and we did very little other than dive on wrecks. Seldom did we come ashore, except to take on fuel and supplies. Dave took everything in stride, even Harold's bad temper. Only when we were out too long, away from civilization, did he become restless. To Dave the romance of the islands had little to do with star-filled nights, azure-blue seas and vistas of curving sand beaches. I would always know what was going on in his head when one of the engines suddenly developed a dangerous something or other.

After one particularly grueling day, we decided to head in for a rest. Dave couldn't have been happier. We anchored the *Virg a Lona* about a hundred yards offshore at Georgetown, Grand Cayman's only real town. There are small settlements such as Hell, Bodden Town and Old Isaacs.

When we rowed into shore in our bathtub-sized skiff, Dave took off.

"Dave," Harold shouted after him. "Be back here at midnight so we can row back to the *Virg a Lona* together."

Dave waved and then disappeared.

Harold looked at me and shrugged.

"If you were twenty-five, you'd be running, too," I remarked.

Both of us grinned and moved to the hotel so we could rent a room and get a real shower. We had laundry to do and chores to take care of. Both of us were looking forward to a restaurant-cooked meal.

We were still in the Beach Club when a little before midnight a wind kicked up. It was soon starting to blow and Harold and I hustled out to the beach to wait for Dave.

Twelve o'clock came and went and still no Dave. Within a half hour the wind was approaching gale force and we knew if we did not reach the *Virg a Lona* soon, she might slip her anchor and wind up on the reef.

Still we hesitated. We expected Dave at any minute.

"Where is he?" Harold hissed between his teeth.

I looked at the water. The wind had turned cold; it was chopping up the waves so they were slapping at one another causing great noise.

Finally Dave was spotted running toward us from the direction of the Beach Club.

"Where the hell have you been?" Harold screamed as we all ran for the dingy.

"Look at this wind! Didn't you know we'd be in trouble?"

We removed our shoes and he was still screaming at him. In fact, he was screaming while we were rowing and bailing, trying to keep that little boat afloat as we were blindly and hopefully moving toward the *Virg a Lona* in the chaotic blackness of the storm.

We prayed the *Virg a Lona* was still there. We prayed just as hard we did not miss her if she was. We had left her just 300 feet offshore, but the way we were being thrust by those waves made our chances of reaching anything seem remote.

Finally . . . there she was . . . ahead of us . . . rolling back and forth with such violence that at times she disappeared behind a wave. When we pulled alongside, the boarding was like gambling a crushed leg against a broken arm. One moment we were even with the boarding ladder, the next we were below the *Virg a Lona's* waterline.

Once aboard, Harold ran to start the engines as Dave and I pulled the dingy aboard, secured it and hauled the anchor. Pulling that anchor under the best of circumstances was a two-man job, but the way the *Virg a Lona* was pitching that night we could have used a half dozen men. Eventually we had it up and secured; I'll never know how we did it.

There was no time for pondering. We ran around to the other side of the island for protection. There is a barrier reef on that side with an opening wide enough for safe passage . . . in the daytime. However, it was black as only black in a storm at night can be.

Moving slowly — I say that as if I thought the *Virg a Lona* had another speed — we headed out to sea.

Looking back, we saw a light and knew it was from a boat. We figured it was Bob Soto's *Cayman Pilot,* which we had seen him move earlier in the evening. Aiming for the light, we picked our way through the reef with Harold at the wheel and Dave and I lying on the bow just on the chance that we might spot trouble before we hit it.

We made it and anchored for the night about 600 feet from the *Cayman Pilot.* Others were not so lucky; their boats were smashed to pieces during the storm. The next day we watched as people walked along the shore picking up pieces of what had been a boat, look at what they had in their hands, then drop it. A pathetic sight.

Harold was still screaming at Dave the next day. When he finally calmed down, I suggested he fly back to Miami to gather some of the parts we needed to maintain our equipment. I figured the weather would keep the ocean choppy for the next several days; we would be beached regardless.

When Dave and I saw Harold off at the airport, he seemed pre-occupied. Since Cuba that was normal and I didn't think much about it until three days later when I received a cable from him. It hit me like a punch in the stomach.

The cable read: "Cannot return to Grand Cayman. Suggest you hire a captain there. Letter and explanation will follow. Shipped parts today. Good luck." It was signed: "Harold."

The dream had faded for Harold. He was concerned about his family. I could understand it because I was going through something of the same thing myself. I, too, had given up home, car, job, and my wife and kids. The difference was I had not wound up in Cuba wondering if I would ever get back. All I knew was of the four who had started with the dream, I was the only one left. Art Hartman had returned to Florida to work with Mel Fisher and Treasure Salvors, but I didn't know that then.

Changes were happening in me. They were subtle at first, mainly because I felt inadequate in any of the particulars of my new profession. As long as Harold was with me, I could take things a little at a time. He was there to back me up or give advice. When he departed, determination took his place.

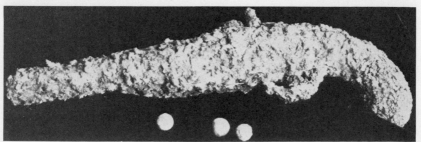

A coral-encrusted pistol, which was taken off a wreck in the Florida Keys in 1967.

(Dick Richmond Photo)

8

LEARNING TO LIVE WITH SHARKS

COMPASSION HAS BEEN SHOWN FOR THE FRANKENSTEIN monster, but seldom have I heard a kind word for his creator, Baron Frankenstein. Well, I have some feeling for the Baron because I was plagued by a similar problem and found myself asking the same question: "What have I done?"

It all started innocently enough when I told Dave to look into the mirror.

"OK," he said. "What am I supposed to see?"

"Our new captain."

Those were the magic words. They did not change him instantly. Like Frankenstein's baby, it took Dave a while to snap his chains. When he did, he turned into the briny old man of the sea. For hours on end he would read books on the ocean; he started picking up some pretty salty talk; then he began giving orders like a French admiral.

"Do this! Do that! Tighten up that line! Run forward and get ready to set the anchor!"

It was amusing watching the metamorphosis from shy young man to Captain Bligh, except I was the only Fletcher Christian aboard. All those orders were being shouted at me.

I began to think I should have taught him how to use the magnetometer and taken over the duties of captain myself. It was just a matter of waiting. I figured his bout with self-importance would pass, and it did, but not before he had the opportunity to use it on the newest member of our crew.

We went to see Bob Soto for suggestions regarding a new hand for the *Virg a Lona*. Bob recommended Mike Ebanks, a twenty-one-year-old islander with a hare lip. Mike talked slowly to compensate for his speech impediment, except when he became excited or angry, then the words erupted in a boil of verbal confusion. From the

58

moment we shook hands, I knew I would sign him on.

As soon as his duties were explained to him and he was introduced to Dave, he made the mistake of asking when he could start. When I told him he had already started, Dave began shouting orders.

Mike rushed to please, yet he did not know to where he was rushing exactly because he did not understand Dave's newly acquired lingo. As a matter of fact, I didn't understand it either.

I think Dave's voice lowered an octave after his appointment. Two thoughts came to mind; either he had a sore throat from screaming all those damn orders, or he felt that an old sea dog should have a rough bark.

I thought, ''Thank God for Mike.'' Two more days of just Dave and me and I would have flown to Miami and wired a cable I would not be returning either.

At first Dave was unsure of himself. He would postpone an order and retire to the head where he kept his books, giving himself time to figure out the right decision. When he emerged, he had made a decision and it was usually the right one. Dave could handle the *Virg a Lona*. When the idea of being captain matured, he turned into a first-class skipper.

Regarding Mike, I knew I had made the right decision in signing him on the first time we pulled in for fuel. The island youngsters, who were in the habit of swarming over the boat as soon as we moored, were run off quickly by Mike. Even with the speech impediment, he had no difficulty making himself understood when he

An anchor from a semi-modern wreck found by Roy Volker, Dave Meinell and Mike Ebanks in the Cayman Islands. (Roy Volker Photo)

wanted to.

Mike quickly adapted to using scuba gear and the things required of him. We were back in business. Months passed and we dug on wreck after wreck. We were finding things but had not yet hit the big paydirt. The work was exhausting yet satisfying in a way because one by one we were eliminating every wreck around Grand Cayman. If a treasure wreck did exist, we knew it was just a matter of time before we found it.

Finally we called a temporary halt to the operation. Dave and I wanted to fly back to St. Louis and see our families as well as report our progress to our investors. In ten days we were back and discovered while we were gone Mike had sanded the *Virg a Lona* and then had stained and painted the boat from bow to stern.

As we inspected her, Mike stood watching us, his eyes shining. Neither of us said a word at first and I could see a fleck of doubt flash over his face. Then I smiled and so did Dave. Both of us clapped him on the back.

"It looks great, Mike," I said.

Dave agreed. "I've never seen the *Virg a Lona* look so good."

Mike flooded with emotion. His chest puffed and he grinned. When he tried to talk, he couldn't quite get it out clearly. So he kind of hummed and pointed to things we might have missed. We circled the boat three times before he was satisfied we had seen everything.

"Come on," I told him, "Dave and I are taking you to the Beach Club for dinner."

When I said this, Mike stopped smiling. "I don't think I should go there," he said.

"Why not?"

"It's too fine."

"Nonsense," I said. "We're going. The three of us are shipmates, aren't we?"

Mike looked from Dave to me uncertainly.

"Well, aren't we?" I persisted.

Mike grinned and ran to change clothes. The evening was a smash for Mike, but only after we left the club. He wasn't comfortable there because he felt he didn't belong. In all the times the three of us went out together in the months to come that never changed.

What did change was Mike's attitude toward Dave and me.

He really became one of us for the first time. Suddenly he seemed to want us to know all about him; his ambitions, his friends, his background.

"I don't want to be a fisherman, Roy," he confided. "Everyone is a fisherman. I want to learn a trade or own my own boat someday.

"My friends understand me when I speak. I have noticed it is too difficult for people who are not my friends to hear me when I speak."

A week after our coming home dinner, Dave was ashore filling our air banks with the compressor we had left with Bob Soto. I was below and Mike was off on an errand. When he returned, he had two of his friends with him. They wanted to come aboard.

"Sorry," Mike said. "Roy is not here and he told me no one is to come aboard when he or Dave is not here."

I heard one of the boys complain to Mike about the quality of his friendship. Mike's response was immediate. "You are my friend, Donald," Mike told him, "but Roy is also my friend. Should I displease one friend so as to please another?"

I didn't hear Donald's response, but he or any other unauthorized person ever came aboard the *Virg a Lona* while Mike was on watch. To me what was more important was I knew Mike thought of Dave and me as friends.

The next time we were ashore because of the weather Mike took me to meet his parents. We walked along the main road from Georgetown, then took a narrow path through the bush. En route Mike didn't say much and the longer we walked, the less sure he seemed he was doing the right thing. As it was, he looked positively miserable by the time we reached his small home, which sat by itself alone in the wilderness.

Mike opened the door and sat me down on a chair in a small living room. Then he disappeared. When he returned he had two very old, wrinkled persons with him.

"Roy, this is my father and my mother," he said.

Getting to my feet, I extended my hand to the old man, who took it and pumped it up and down twice very vigorously, then let it drop as if he had primed an old hand-cranked water pump. With that he looked at me smiling, seemingly waiting for conversation or water to flow. I was never sure which.

"Mother and Father," Mike said, "this is my friend from the United States, Roy Volker."

Once the pleasantries were over Mike whisked me out of his home. Again he was uncomfortable for reasons he never explained and I never asked. I did know the meeting had taken place in a gesture of friendship on his part.

While I was in the Caymans, the islands still were not suffering under taxes of any kind. King George III supposedly granted this amnesty in perpetuity after Cayman islanders saved his son from the Wreck of the Seven Sails at Grand Cayman's East End in a place called Gun Bay. Some people refer to the eighteenth century incident as the Wreck of the Ten Sails, some Seven. It could be either one because we uncovered many more than ten wrecks in that watery graveyard.

It was Mike who suggested we search there. Gun Bay is at the eastern tip of the island about twenty miles from Georgetown. It was he who told us the story of how Gun Bay had been used by pirates, who would sail out to prey on English shipping.

To resolve the situation it was decided by the British to wipe out the rascals once and for all. A fleet of seven British warships (ten for those who like bigger numbers) set sail for Gun Bay. A point was sent out by the admiral of the fleet with orders to block the entrance to the bay. If the pirates were there, the captain of the ship was told to fire a cannon.

As ordered, the captain of the point vessel sailed his ship to the opening into the bay. Suddenly he was caught in the treacherous current that flowed through the reef. That current, combined with giant waves, made it impossible for the helmsman to control the ship. She was helpless.

In panic the captain had a warning shot fired. The other six ships thinking they had the pirates trapped sailed in for the kill. Before any of them could grasp the situation, they were absorbed by the sea and sucked to their deaths in the East End graveyard.

That's where we headed. When we arrived, the weather was calm and the water like glass. Taking advantage of the situation, we worked outside the reefs. At night we moved inside for safe anchorage.

Basically we were interested in old wrecks; they promised more chance of treasure than the modern ones. However, we passed up nothing. It was on a modern wreck we found our first gold.

Mike and I were picking up some brass porthole covers from a schooner when I lifted one and saw a United States $10 gold piece with an 1890 date. Next to it was a United States $2.50 gold piece with an 1891 date. Neither was in mint condition, but at least it was a find.

Roy Volker looks at a modern victim at Gun Bay on Grand Cayman Island.
                                                        (Dave Meinell Photo)

Moving the *Virg a Lona* over the site, we anchored it and used our propwash blowers on the wreck. What gold there was on that wreck we had already found.

After that we gave modern wreckage careful attention. It paid off three days later. Dave found three English gold sovereigns and Mike found two. They were all dated about 1890.

Outside the reef it was impossible to use the mag. There were anchors, chain and modern wreckage scattered all over the place. Since the mag responds to ferrous material, electronically searching the seaward part of the reef would have been like looking for an aircraft carrier in a swimming pool.

Of course, we did not need search equipment. We had plenty to investigate just eyeballing the wrecks. Yet working outside the reefs had its drawbacks, even with the tons of wreckage over which to pick. That was part of the problem; we had a wealth of junk.

There were other problems as well. Even when the ocean was calm, working too close to the reefs was risky. A swell could carry a diver onto the coral, which was infested with sea urchins. The urchins have quills that will penetrate a wet suit easily.

The biggest hassle was with sharks. They were everywhere, and Dave would go chasing off to kill them. Dave was a fantastic companion except for his two ambitions. The first was to court every woman he met, the second was to kill every shark he saw. Both wasted a lot of time and they were the only things over which we ever argued.

One of his girlfriends wound up in the water when I told him not to bring her aboard. Which caused some strong feelings for about ten minutes.

In spite of our occasional disagreements, which were never serious, Dave would back me up on everything whether it was a barroom brawl with half the British fleet or in the water with a pack of sharks. What's more, he did his share.

I had to watch two things with Dave: We had irreparable problems with the boat and a dangerous shortage of food only when Dave felt we had been away from town too long to suit him. Knowing that, I was able to keep a tight rein on things.

Regarding the sharks: I didn't mind him ridding the area of those potential mankillers; but he wasted valuable time.

We noticed their presence mostly in late afternoon and early morning. At midday we were not troubled with them too often, yet something had to be done.

"Sharks don't like dead sharks," Mike said.

I had heard that before. Fishermen are not too concerned with sharks, as are divers. I had heard about divers using dead sharks to frighten away other sharks. I didn't believe it, guessing it was just wishful thinking on the part of those challenging the ocean on its own terms.

"It's true," Mike assured us.

It would cost nothing to give it a try, so the day Mike suggested it, we baited two large hooks and caught two sharks that night. Being hooked, the sharks could not swim the way they must in order to force air through their gills, so when we hauled them aboard in the morning, they were dead.

Carrying the sharks out to the wreck we planned to work, we attached a float to the end of a fifty-foot line, the other end of which we hooked to an anchor. That accomplished, we attached the life-less bodies of the two sharks under the float and let them dangle a few feet from the bottom. After that we were no longer harrassed by sharks on the outside of the reef.

The three of us had diametrically different points of view about sharks; you already know what Dave would do; I would watch and clip them with a hammer if they came too close; Mike would run. Mike's attitude was the most dangerous to himself, and to us. So I tried to cure him.

Most of Mike's young life had been spent in the ocean or on it. His fear of sharks was innate. At the first glimpse of one he would head for the boat full throttle without once looking back.

On the bottom of the sea with someone with you a diver has a good chance. Alone those chances are reduced.

The first time I caught him turning tail and swimming wildly for the boat, I explained he would be better off if he worked his way back, keeping an eye on the shark while doing it. There are ways a person can protect himself, I said, if he watches his adversary.

"How?" he wanted to know.

"You can shout, push your purge valve to shoot a burst of air bubbles at him, slap the water with one of your fins. You can even swim toward him as if you're going to attack."

Mike regarded me narrowly and wiped the water from his nose. "OK," he said. "Next time I will stay."

A few days later he had his chance. We anchored outside the reefs and while Dave worked on our ailing starboard engine, Mike and I grabbed our masks, fins and a chipping hammer. By this time we had acquired a Boston whaler to replace the bathtub-sized skiff. Using the whaler, we anchored near the reef and jumped in to work a wreck site.

Until then we had had to ignore this wreck because it was right on the reef. Now the water was dead calm and we would not have to worry about being pushed into the jagged coral by a sneaky wave.

The reef was home for thousands of fish. The wreck was semi-modern and offered protection for thousands more. It was shelter for those fish who could find shelter and a feeding ground for carnivores who darted in to snap up the unwary.

We were free diving and the morning passed into afternoon. Mostly we were fanning potholes, trying to find something that might have fallen into one. In one I discovered a solid block of metal that felt like silver when I first picked it up; it turned out to be coral-encrusted iron. It was the disappointment of the day. I should say it would have been the disappointment of the day if it had not been for the sharks and Mike.

Four blue sharks appeared out of nowhere. By the time Mike moved behind me and pointed in their direction, I already had them spotted.

We surfaced. "Take it easy," I told Mike. Looking at the whaler, I judged it to be about two city blocks away. "We'll work our way back to the whaler and keep a close watch on 'em."

As we finned our way to safety, I asked Mike to hand me the hammer. The blues were starting to circle too close for comfort. No hammer.

"Mike," I snapped.

No answer. Looking over my shoulder, I found myself alone. Then I saw Mike. He was heading for the whaler full speed . . . full speed with my chipping hammer.

The blues were large. Too large. I was afraid I looked like a meal. I would see one and then another. Suddenly one or the other would disappear from view. My flesh started to crawl and I peered at the bottom trying to pick out something I might use as a weapon.

There was nothing. Here I was in a junkyard and I had to be swimming over a spot that had nothing but beautiful white sand.

Being on the surface, I was vulnerable. As they began to close in on me, it was difficult to keep them all in sight. I would be lying if I said that fear didn't grasp me by the throat when that circle began to close.

Again I glanced over my shoulder and saw Mike pulling himself aboard the whaler. "Good," I thought, "once he starts the motor, it will frighten off the blues."

No motor. The blues were beginning to make aggressive passes. I kept watching them and waiting for Mike as I worked myself toward the whaler. Again I glanced over my shoulder. What I saw made me wild with rage, and I let out a shout even Dave could hear. Mike was standing in the boat trying to light a cigarette with a book of damp matches.

"Damn you," I screamed, then looked at the blues.

Mike almost jumped out of the boat.

"Get that damn thing started, you S.O.B."

The sharks were getting close enough to kiss.

"Pick me up," I yelled at the top of my lungs.

Mike started the motor at my first scream and as he headed my way, the blues departed. When I pulled myself aboard, I wanted to slap the hell out of him. Instead I screamed until I thought he was going to cry. I called him every kind of coward imaginable — and he took it.

Later that night, when we had pulled back into the bay to anchor for the night, Mike came back to the stern where I was lying on my back making mental conversation with the stars.

"You still mad, Roy?" he asked.

"No. Disappointed."

Mike sat cross-legged next to me for a time without saying a word.

"You hate me?" he said.

"I thought you would stand your ground."

"Fear."

"One of these days you're going to get hit doing what you did today."

"I will stand my ground next time," he promised.

But he never did.

Mike Ebanks with a dead shark used to frighten away the live ones.   (Roy Volker Photo)

9

SWEPT OUT TO SEA

REGARDING THE WRECK OF THE SEVEN SAILS, we found a lot of cannons and grog bottles but no loose change. This told me that the English were fighters and drinkers but did not have much in the way of spending money. Which, as I think about it, is probably what made them want to fight and drink.

At any rate, our operation on the outside of the reef came to a close when the weather changed. We moved into the lagoon, where the water was calm. It was a good thing we had wrecks on which to pick on the inside because until the weather changed for the better that was where we would be staying.

There was a lot of modern wreckage, yet despite that we were able to use the mag for the first time since our arrival at Gun Bay. We found five wrecks buried deep under the sand. Three turned out to be turtle boats, which yielded a lot of bones as well as a few large water jugs, some knives, forks and spoons. One wreck was a small merchant ship (circa 1800) and it was from this wreck we received our biggest thrill.

One look told us we had not uncovered a treasure galleon. It was much too small, but in the first hole we blew with our propwash we found six milled Spanish Carolus dollars with an effigy of Charles IV looking like a Roman emperor. I would not see coins exactly like these again until 1974 when Dick Richmond and I happened on what appeared to be a wreck on the Missouri River.*

It was almost dark when we blew that first hole so we had to call it quits for the evening. To be sure we wouldn't lose our place we stayed anchored over the wreck that night. We attempted to sleep,

*See ''Treasure Under Your Feet'' by Volker and Richmond.

A Carolus dollar taken from Missouri River wreck.
(Dick Richmond Photo)

but were so excited the best we could manage was to keep our eyes shut and keep quiet.

At daybreak we started without breakfast. Since the bow anchor and the stern anchors were already set, we were ready to go. With the first hole already blown, we wanted to redirect the propwash. To do that we shortened one of the stern anchor lines as we let out the other, swinging the stern around. This way we didn't have to reanchor every time we wanted to blow a hole.

An airlift sucks the sand off the bottom like a vacuum, and the current carries the sand away. Any heavy object, such as a coin, will be sucked up, too, but will fall immediately behind or to the side of where you are working.

With a propwash the system is different. It blows the sand off a wreck, digging a funnel-shaped hole as much as six feet deep to perhaps fifty feet in diameter in five minutes. The sand is blown away but any heavy objects such as coins tumble to the center of the hole. It is a much more practical tool for the treasure hunter than the airlift. And since there is almost nothing of the ships remaining except rubble in tropical waters, usually nothing of value is destroyed.

After we blew the first hole of the morning, we made a mad scramble to see what was at the bottom of it. Nothing. Again we moved the stern, this time about six feet to the other side of the original hole. The engines were revved and we blew our third hole.

Dave found a silver tea strainer and Mike uncovered our seventh Carolus dollar. We blasted holes on that wreck for four days and found four more coins. We did uncover some medallions, a small cross, several belt buckles, pottery and the usual ship fittings. I had enough experience by then to know we were not going to retire on what we were finding. So the wreck was abandoned.

The fifth buried wreck in the lagoon proved to be the oldest we would find in the Caymans. From it we took a large number of artifacts and a few coins and a perfect onion skin bottle (circa 1650).

We also uncovered several unbroken amphoras, a heap of grape shot and seven four thousand-pound cannons. These cannons matched six I had found earlier in shallow water near the entrance through the reef. Later I found seven more. They were about a mile away buried almost on shore, and these matched the other thirteen. We guessed the Spanish had salvaged the ship themselves.

We were running out of wrecks to work and still we were trapped in the lagoon. Inside it was flat as a pond, but outside the sea was rough. Waves were crashing over the reef overfilling the lagoon. To

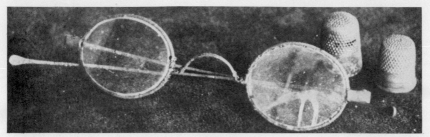

Thimbles and eye glasses taken off a wreck in the Caymans by Volker.
(Dick Richmond Photo)

escape, the water would rush through the hole in the reef creating a dangerous rip current. Trying to sail out through the channel would be suicidal.

I did not like our situation, yet there was nothing I could do about it. We rechecked the wrecks but spent most of our time snorkeling, trying to spot something we might have overlooked.

At night I gave my waking hours to re-examining the research on the *Maravillas*. It was becoming more intriguing to me. I knew the fleet had departed from Havana on January 1. Taking into account the current in the Straits of Florida, by the night of January 4 the ships even with headwinds would have sailed way beyond Cay Sal Bank.

I had been to Cay Sal Bank on that first trip years before if you recall. I remembered something about it that had not occurred to me before. The scores of uninhabited islands making up the bank are surrounded by water deep enough for the most part to accommodate the eighteen-foot drafts of the galleons. There are some coral heads and some sandbanks but not so many as around Red Riding Rocks and on Little Bahama Bank, on which there stands the lonely sentinel, Memory Rock. Los Mimbres had to be one of those two. Cay Sal Bank was out.

There were bits and pieces of information supplied by the men who had attempted to salvage the *Maravillas* in the months and years afterwards. From their letters I attempted to pull some magical clue that would show me where they had been searching.

The information was often ambiguous, or perhaps I read things into their words never intended. Yet there seemed to be a conflict of information even regarding the depth of water in which Orellana's galleon sank. It was as deep as eighty feet and as shallow as twenty-five.

When I finally put the information away at night, I would rub my eyes trying to picture the sunken ship, or a break in the weather so we could finally sail out of Gun Bay and on to another project.

One afternoon I found the remains of a ship that had gone down in the channel. Returning to the *Virg a Lona*, I donned a tank and started over the side. I wanted a better look.

"Roy," Mike warned, "watch that channel. Bad current."

Nodding, I dropped beneath the surface. After several days of boredom, I could not wait to inspect the new find. The *Virg a Lona* was anchored about 500 feet from the channel and I knew if I watched my air supply, I would have no problems.

As soon as I neared the channel, I could feel the current. To keep my bearings I was working my way along the bottom, hand over hand, from one piece of wreckage to another. It did not take me long to decide the wreck was probably less than seventy years old, yet I was finding things: spoons, bowls, a copper pot. It was not a treasure wreck but the picking was easy and it was something to do.

Returning to the *Virg a Lona,* I unloaded my finds and grabbed an artifact bag. Mike and Dave were taking a nap and I saw no need to awaken them. Checking my air, I figured I had enough left for another twenty minutes.

As I worked along the bottom, I suddenly lost my sense of direction. It only took a moment. Turning to reorient myself, I had the sensation the bottom was being pulled out from underneath me. It seemed to be rushing by. I was caught in the current.

For a short time I tried to fin against it, but it was useless and I knew I was being swept out to sea. Surfacing, I yelled but the waves crashing against the reef muffled my voice. There was no one on deck.

"No one will know," I thought.

There was nothing I could do but let the current take me. I was wearing a wet suit jacket and had my mask, snorkel and fins. I knew I would not drown. Jettisoning my tank, I watched it drop out of sight into the deep water.

I had two fears: Being permanently lost and sharks — it was late afternoon and I was being swept out so far that no one would ever find me.

Bobbing like a cork, the water seemed to be carrying me south along the coast. I felt as if I were miles offshore. After a few hours I noticed I was no longer being towed.

I had been in the water a long time and my legs were numb. I started to swim. After about a half hour I could tell I was making headway. Another hour of swimming and I entered a new current; this one helped me.

Night was falling when I reached the beach. I was exhausted and my arms and legs did not want to move. Had it not been for the fact I was in the best shape I had been in since my days in the ring, I don't believe I could have forced myself to move. Of course, if I hadn't been in such excellent physical condition, I probably would not have had to worry about it.

I laid on the beach and rested for a long while, then I walked through the bush of this uninhabited part of Grand Cayman until I found a road. Eventually I located some islanders who drove me back to East End and Gun Bay. There a fisherman took me aboard his boat and ran me out to the *Virg a Lona*.

I knew what was happening to me, but Dave and Mike did not.

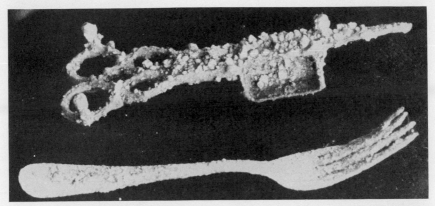

A candle snuffer and a fork found on a wreck in the Bahamas by Roy Volker in 1969.
(Dick Richmond Photo)

They were frantic, certain I had drowned yet unable to do anything except wait. They were so happy to see me I was afraid they were going to kiss me.

The next day the ocean calmed and we sailed away from that watery graveyard forever. The impression it left on me was indelible. Of all the dangers in the sea, the current is the one I fear the most. There is no way to fight against it.

I've been asked countless times why a man would keep pursuing that rainbow when there were so many obstacles. We were finding things. Not much, but enough for us to keep hoping.

Then, too, we were experiencing the unique rewards of living. Each day, from morning until night, we saw beauty and drama, the likes of which we could never enjoy in the city. More importantly, we were conquering challenges of a very basic nature. That must be good for the soul, because it felt so right.

Among the imponderables was the companionship men find only when they share a common goal, the friendship of depending upon one another for life and food, of caring for other human beings in a way untainted by petty quarrels, greed or jealousies.

There were no bad days, only some that left a deeper impression on me than others. To relive those times, I believe I would endure everything again just as it happened.

10
GOLDEN OPPORTUNITY

BACK IN GEORGETOWN EACH OF US went our separate ways for three days, playing tourist after all those weeks at East End. The closest I came to water was the hotel shower.

On our second night back John Cumber invited me for dinner and cocktails at the Beach Club. At the time the club showed movies once a week. The island administrator and I stayed for the show and afterwards sat chatting into the wee hours of the morning as we watched the bartender performing his own special kind of magic, concocting drinks that had become island favorites.

Occasionally I noticed John would start to say something and then would change his mind. Finally he asked, "Roy, what are you really doing here?"

It seemed like a strange question since we had been breaking our backs for months trying to uncover every wreck we came across. "Trying to get rich, John," I answered. "I'm looking for treasure just like I said I was. Why do you ask?"

John studied me in silence for what seemed like a long time, as if he were trying to make up his mind about something. Then he said, "It seems, old boy, that our intelligence people (British) and yours (the FBI) have received information that a man high in American politics who swindled millions in your country has been sending the money out of the United States. Somehow it ended up in Jamaica.

"From what our people have been telling me, gold has been purchased with the money and huge amounts of it have been made to resemble bars of Spanish gold. The bars are to be passed off as treasure recovered from a sunken Spanish galleon."

John removed a pen from his pocket and on a napkin drew a

72

symbol. "Each bar will have a number of different markings. However, they will all have one in common that will look like this."

The symbol John had drawn resembled the mint mark of Lima, Peru.

I listened in fascination. Three days earlier I had been swept out to sea trying to pick junk off a wreck and now I was about to be told I was suspect of being a possible go-between in a million-dollar gold scheme.

It is difficult to describe what was going through my mind because the thoughts ranged from larcenous to indignation. As I turned out, I decided that being indignant did not fit my character, and my honesty at that time was not to be put to the test.

John continued. "From what we have been able to find out, the gold bars are supposed to show up here in Grand Cayman. We have been wondering for some time if you were sent here as the plant."

"No, John, I wasn't," I assured him.

John pretended to believe me. "Good," he said. "But if anyone approaches you about it, will you let me know?"

I nodded and, with that, the conversation returned to things more mundane.

Strangely enough when I finally was approached about the gold, I was already back in the United States, and living in St. Louis. A man in Florida contacted me and asked if I could dispose of large amounts of gold. I assured him I could if the price was right.

A meeting was arranged. I was sent a round trip ticket to Miami, where I was picked up at the airport and driven to a motel in the Keys. I was told the gold was in bar form hidden somewhere in the West Indies.

"There's about one ton of it," he told me. "It was removed from a treasure galleon."

Remembering the story John Cumber had told me, I picked up a pencil laying next to the phone and drew the symbol John had shown me on the telephone directory.

My contact almost fell off his chair.

"How did you know that?" he demanded.

I told him the story as John had told it to me. When I finished, the man handed me two $100 bills and had me driven back to the airport. And that was the last I heard of that.

The talk with John Cumber occurred on the second night of our three-day holiday. The third night would lead us to the next phase of our operation.

It was Sunday and I was back at the Beach Club for dinner. It was there that I was introduced to a weather-worn American with leathery skin and a vise-like grip. I'll call him Hale.

Hale operated a small fishing and diving business on Little Cayman, which is about sixty-three miles northeast of Grand Cayman. He catered to those who sought solitude on their vacations. If they lodged with Hale, they also sought discomfort.

The man was pleasant enough until he discovered I was a treasure hunter and I legally had the right to work wrecks in all the Caymans.

Glaring at me, he said, "I make the rules in Little Cayman. And nobody does any treasure hunting there without my permission."

I smiled. "You must have something good to get this mean about it."

"Just keep away if you don't want trouble."

I stopped smiling. This was definitely not the way to start the week, but the previous one had been so lousy, I figured, what the hell!

"Hale," I said slowly, so he could not mistake my meaning. "You just made up my mind for me. Little Cayman is next." With that I walked away.

Dave, Mike and I spent the next two days taking on water and supplies and in getting the *Virg a Lona* ready for our next effort.

In the final two hours of preparation, Dave disappeared below. I knew what he was doing. I had seen him plotting and replotting the course on the chart the night before . . . and the night before that. He knew every inch of the coast of Grand Cayman, but he had never been the pilot on an open-water crossing before.

When we were ready to start, he acted as if he could do it in his sleep. He was cool and straight and his hands did not clench the wheel. However, his eyes flicked back and forth from the chart to the compass.

Running at ten knots, the voyage from Georgetown to Little Cayman is about six hours. When after five hours, we still did not see the island, each of us became quiet.

I could see the same question in Mike and Dave's faces: Where the hell is that island? Another hour went by and still no island. All of us stood silently scanning the horizon.

It was Dave who saw it first. When he did, he let out a whoop that almost ripped open the cabin roof. "There it is," he screamed. "Dead ahead, right where it's supposed to be."

The three of us pounded one another on the back as if we were the first to circle the globe. Magellan could not have done it better.

However, Mr. Hale was not as happy to have us as we were to be there. We had barely dropped anchor in the lagoon that bordered Hale's wilderness resort when one of the two islanders whom he employed was out in a skiff to greet us with a message.

"Mr. Hale wants to see you," he called.

"I'm too busy," I responded. "If he wants to see me, tell him to come out to the boat."

The islander took off. Twenty minutes later Hale was motoring out to see me accompanied by his two men. When they arrived, I was on deck cleaning my .270 rifle. I'm an old poker player and I know when it's time to bluff. However, in this case I had a pat hand and no blowhard was going to make me take a second look.

Hale was all eyes when he saw the rifle, which had a scope mounted on it. He asked if he could come aboard. Before he uttered a word, I knew he would be singing a different tune.

"Well, I see you made it,"
he chirped.

I nodded.

"I thought maybe we could
make a deal."

"No deal. If you have anything
here, I'll find it."

"I could save you time and
money," Hale said. "I'll point
out the wrecks and you won't
have to spend time searching."

That kind of talk I understood.
I told him, "OK, Hale, anything
you show us that yields treasure
of any type, I'll cut you in for ten
per cent. But whatever we find
without your help, you get
zero."

"Fair enough," he said,
smiling. We shook hands to seal
the bargain.

Hale had four wrecks, none of

*A goblet found on a wreck in
the Cayman Islands.*
(Dick Richmond Photo)

which amounted to anything.
In fact the most interesting part about the flat, narrow Little Cayman
is that it once was a pirate stronghold. In the early 1700s the English
decided to rid this island of its thieving inhabitants.

At daybreak one morning, warships bombarded the small pirate
village. To escape, the pirates and their families dashed across the
island in an attempt to reach their ships, which were anchored in
a bay on the other side.

The pirate ships had already been captured. Waiting for the
fleeing people were more than a hundred British marines. No priso-
ners were taken and that part of the island is still called Bloody Bay.
We found the remains of two burned wrecks in Bloody Bay, but there
was nothing on either one.

In fact, we found nothing of value at Little Cayman, but it occurred
to me then, as it has many times since, a man with a good metal
detector might find a great deal buried on that island. Since it was
a pirate stronghold, they surely would have buried whatever wealth
they had for safekeeping.

If it indeed was buried, those who did the planting would not have
had time to dig anything up the day of Bloody Bay. So it would still
be where they had left it more than 250 years ago.

By the time we arrived on Little Cayman, Mike had become a
house mother. He hated sloppiness and would storm every time
Dave would eat and leave the plate in the sink. It all came to a head
one day, after we found the third of Hale's wrecks. We were all
working hard and were biting to get at it.

At breakfast, Dave had eaten and run, leaving his cereal bowl for

Roy Volker holds Spanish cobs, English gold sovereigns, a silver cross with rough diamonds, and a gold nugget — treasure taken from several wrecks off the Florida coast.

(Dick Richmond Photo)

Mike to clean. At noon Mike was a little testy and refused to join in on the conversation. Then when Dave left a mess at the lunch table, Mike blew up.

"OK, you guys," he fumed, "if you don't make your beds, and pick up your socks and stop leaving your dishes in the sink, I'm going to quit this job."

When Mike exploded, Dave was suited up and ready to re-enter the water. He grinned and grabbed his spear gun before going over the side. Five minutes later he was back with a grouper at the end of his spear.

"Hey, Mike," he yelled. "Clean this for dinner, will you?"

Before Mike could scream at him, Dave had slipped beneath the water again. Worse than cleaning dishes, Mike hated cleaning fish and Dave knew it.

That night we had fried grouper for dinner and Dave cleaned the

Supper for a hungry crew.

(Don Paule Photo)

dishes. When Dave left his breakfast plate the next morning, Mike didn't grumble a bit. There was some sort of moral victory there I still have not been able to puzzle out.

We had been away from Georgetown a couple of weeks by then and the night after the dinner of grouper and bean salad, Dave came out on deck where I was lying.

"We're running short of supplies," Dave informed me.

"We'll eat fish," I responded.

"Water's down, too."

"Looks like rain," I said.

"Did you notice how that starboard engine seems to be acting up?" Dave said, seriously. "I think it's dangerous to run it that way."

"We'll just have to run it then until it falls apart."

Sighing, Dave started to move away.

"Dave," I said, "we'll be in Cayman Brac pretty soon. There's a settlement there."

"When?"

"A week, maybe less. Depends on what we find here."

Dave nodded and went to his bunk. That was the last I heard about low food and water and engine problems for a while.

11

SILVER REMNANTS OF BLOODY BAY

WE HAD A METAL DETECTOR and used it on our next project, but it was not like the sophisticated units available today.*

Leaving Little Cayman, we sailed south five miles to Cayman Brac, which is a cliff rising out of the sea. The other two islands are flat as flapjacks.

Cayman Brac interested me, not because it was littered with wrecks, but because of a story I had heard related by an old fisherman.

It was a story of a storm and it made my flesh crawl. In a month I would be living through a similar kind of hell, but I had no way of knowing that when we sailed in and anchored off the island.

The old fisherman's descriptions were vivid. "We could smell the storm brewing," he recalled, "long before it hit. Cayman Brac had many people on it when I lived there in the summer of 1932.

"We tried to prepare for what we knew would be coming, but there is not much one can do when the sea is so angry. The women and children and most of the men sought refuge in the caves. I would have been there, too, except my old mother had pain in her legs and could not climb. We took shelter in the rocks away from the wind.

"When the storm came, it was night. Midnight. The wind screamed. I had never heard such noise. I put my hands over my ears and still I could hear it screaming.

"By 1:30 great waves were crashing on the beach. Whooomp!" he croaked, and slapped his hands on the bar where we were sitting. "Whoomp . . . whoomp . . . whoomp . . .

"Everything on the beach was crushed. And when the waves destroyed something, the sea took it away. The sea scrubbed our

*See "Treasure Under Your Feet" by Volker and Richmond.

78

dwellings from the earth.

"The waves grew larger. Water spilled into some of the caves. My wife, my daughter were in one of them. They drowned along with a hundred others."

The old man wept as he spoke. "For days after the storm passed we were burying our dead in the cemetery next to the cove."

He paused as if that were the end of the story. Then his tone changed; the unhappy memory was replaced by something else. "A few weeks after the hurricane," he went on, "some children were playing on the beach near the cemetery and found some odd-shaped stones. Everyone thought they were stones. Heavy stones. Until a young seaman saw them. Captain Foster was his name.

"Captain Foster recognized the stones as blackened Spanish pieces of eight. He asked the children where they had found them. When he was taken there, he began to dig.

"Almost at once he found more. Quickly the word spread that the stones were silver. Valuable. Everyone on the island was digging on that beach.

"Before the day was over more than 500 had been found. On the second day less than 100 more were uncovered. On the third perhaps thirty, perhaps less.

"Everyone except Foster and his good fellow gave up. They took a wooden box and removed its bottom. In its place they put a screen made of layers of chicken wire. Carefully shoveling the sand into the box, another 500 coins were found. Eventually, they, too, gave up."

The first time I heard this story I surmised it was the unhappy ramblings of an old man. It may or may not have had a basis in reality. It also occurred to me it was a story for tourists since he was relating it to a group of visiting Americans; I just happened to be in the crowd.

Yet there was so much sincerity in the way he spoke, I checked out what he had related. There was a hurricane in the summer of 1932, I discovered quickly enough. However, I wasn't able to verify the treasure tale. Then I bumped into another old fisherman. He, too, had lived through the horror of Cayman Brac. He related the details in much the same way, adding one very, very important word: gold. Three gold coins had been found, too.

I was sure the beach had long since been cleaned of any treasure. I was interested because I knew a money beach with coins scattered the way these had been usually meant a wreck offshore. If there was a ship, then silver and gold coins could be laying in potholes all over the place.

Arriving at Cayman Brac early in the afternoon, we anchored the *Virg a Lona* in a peaceful cove and took the whaler ashore. We needed supplies, which gave us an opportunity to visit several small stores to make our acquaintance with the friendly islanders.

During our rounds, I met an American couple who owned and operated a small resort on the island. They were kind enough to invite us to a party planned for that evening.

We took the supplies back to the boat, then washed, shaved and changed clothes. Mike, bless his generous heart, volunteered to stay aboard and keep an eye on everything.

Why we were ever invited to the party, I'll never know. We had been out several weeks. After diving all day and working on greasy engines half the night, we must have looked pretty sorry when the American couple first saw us. We were lucky, because the evening was delightful.

Dave became romantically involved with one of the local beauties and soon disappeared, a common practice with him whenever we were ashore. Me? Well, I entered into small-change talk with some of the other guests. The conversation centered around the money beach. It was a blow when none of the islanders at the party were familiar with the story.

However, one person suggested I visit an elderly man who lived on the other side of Cayman Brac. He was almost eighty, I was informed, and had lived on the island since he quit his life as a sailor.

As soon as I could leave without offending my hosts, I departed to find the old seaman. He lived in a small house in a grove of coconut palms. I found it and knocked on the door. No answer. I knocked again. I heard stirring and waited.

The old man who answered must have been big when he was young. When I saw him, he was thin and a little stoop-shouldered from age. Yet he carried himself as a man does who had rubbed elbows with danger and had emerged the better for it.

He smiled a welcome.

"My name is Roy Volker," I said.

"Captain Foster," he introduced himself, and invited me to take a seat on the veranda.

The name did not register immediately, or I would have known he would have been well aware of the fishermen's story. When I finished telling it, his lined face broke into a smile.

"I am the one who found most of those coins. What can I tell you that would be of help?"

Captain Foster! The name finally rang a bell. Of course! I could not believe my good fortune. The man who had dug up the treasure was sitting in front of me.

He assured me the story was true and would be happy to show me exactly where the money beach was located. We had a drink and agreed to meet the next morning.

As I walked away, my mind was filled with the hope that perhaps the search finally would be over. Had the 1932 hurricane washed the coins ashore? Was there a Spanish ship lying just offshore? Were the bones of a galleon or a nao* lying there covered with sand just waiting to be picked clean?

The questions flooded my head and would not leave. I spent most of the night on deck looking at the stars. When I was finally able to lie

*Naos were freighters about the size of galleons.

down and shut my eyes, sleep would not come. When it did, it was restless.

Early the next morning Captain Foster was waiting for me when I pulled the whaler ashore. We walked to a beach from which he claimed he had taken the coins. For more than an hour we stood and talked. When he departed, we shook hands and I told him if we did uncover a treasure that amounted to anything substantial, I would be generous toward him.

We anchored the boat off the beach pointed out to me by Captain Foster. Then I motored ashore with our metal detector and started working the beach in a very tight pattern. The sun was incredible but I kept at it. After three hours, I heard a faint hum.

Dropping to my knees, I carefully started scooping sand with a garden trowel I had brought with me. In a few seconds I uncovered a blackened cob coin, a dated piece of eight in perfect condition. It had been struck in the Lima mint. The date was 700, which meant 1700 as Lima coins often carried only the last three digits.

At that moment I was hit by a bad case of the Cayman Brac treasure fever. I screamed and saw two heads pop up on the *Virg a Lona*. Holding the coin and the metal detector above my head, I yelled, "I found it . . . I found it."

Dave dove into the water and swam ashore. The way the two of us carried on, an onlooker would have thought we had uncovered King Solomon's mines instead of one coin.

Dave took over with the metal detector and I motored back to the *Virg a Lona* to get out of the sun and to drink enough water to keep from becoming dehydrated. I was not back on board long enough to sit down when I heard Dave yelling.

Back into the whaler I went and motored in as if an alligator was after me. Dave came running up, talking so fast I could hardly understand him. However, I did understand the coin he dropped in my hand. Mine had been an eight real; his was only a four, but it was as pretty as the first. The date was 1701.

The rest of the day was spent on the beach. After a time Mike swam ashore and joined us in a fruitless search. It was nightfall before we motored back and stuffed ourselves with fried grouper.

The night was beautiful and conversation lasted for hours. At last we had proof we were on a spot where treasure did exist at one time. We discussed our next approach in the hunt and decided to give up working the beach. There were probably more coins there, but if we were to find a pile of them, it would be in the water. We agreed the best procedure would be to swim the offshore area and eyeball the site first. Something — anything — ballast, cannon, an anchor could lead us to the remains of a ship.

That night I had no difficulty sleeping. The next morning, after a light breakfast, the three of us donned flippers and face masks and snorkeled in close to the beach. The water was clear enough to see 200 feet in every direction.

Spreading out, we worked the water just off the money beach. The sand was deep, and now and again one of us would dive to inspect a coral formation, or fan a crevice by hand.

Slowly, we worked our way out into deeper water. We were diving in about twenty feet of water when I found our third coin in a pothole. It was a coral-encrusted piece of eight.

Fanning a few more times, I marked the spot with my chipping hammer and headed for the surface. Dave and I put on tanks and swam to where I had found the coin. We fanned more potholes and uncovered three more encrusted coins. When we depleted our air, we made for the *Virg a Lona*.

Now we were more excited than ever. Here we were in twenty to twenty-five feet of water and finding coins. Surely we had a wreck. I decided to use the mag to see if we could pinpoint it.

Putting out the torpedo head, we sailed into deeper water to tune the instrument. The area was clean of ferrous material and it functioned perfectly. Once we were sure, Dave headed in as close to shore as possible so we could run a pattern parallel to the beach.

At the completion of every pass, he would turn and move out about twenty feet, then run the same pattern. Hour after hour we made one pass after another without the slightest change in our readings. The mag was steady as a rock . . . there was nothing there to interfere with it.

Eventually we passed over the area where we had picked up the coins. Still no wreck. By late afternoon we were working in water fifty feet deep and still we did not get one reading that even suggested wreckage.

We anchored for the night in the spot where we stopped our search. The next day we would take it from there and continue looking. I did not say anything to the others, but I was concerned. It was difficult for me to believe even the worst storm could cause the ocean to boil enough to throw coins on shore from fifty feet of water.

Early the following morning we were at it again. Since we would be working in deeper water, I attached a wing to the sensing head to make it dive; it would travel just a few feet off the bottom. Using the fathometer to check the depth, we would play out as much cable as needed to take the sensing head down.

Morning approached midday and we were moving into deeper and deeper water. Then in eighty-five feet of water we got a hit. I yelled and Mike threw a buoy. We made another pass and again we got a hit at the same spot. The marking buoys were less than fifteen feet apart.

Anchoring over the area, Dave and I broke out our diving gear. At the depth at which we would be going we figured we would have about fifteen minutes of bottom time. A decompression stop would be required. We checked our underwater watches. We would have to gauge our time closely. In fifteen minutes, however, we were sure to find whatever had caused the reading. At eighty-five feet the bottom would be mostly hardpan. Anything down there would be at least partly visible.

I grabbed my chipping hammer and Dave grabbed a bang stick (shark killer). Over the side and down the anchor line we went. Slowly we worked our way down, stopping several times to equalize the pressure on our ears.

As we descended, the water became colder and darker. We hit bottom together. In front of us was a large anchor and a pile of chain. One look told us they were not off a galleon. My guess was that the anchor had not been used before 1800. We looked around for a few minutes, then headed for the surface.

At forty feet we paused for a short decompression stop. We were hanging on the anchor line when we received company — four large brown sharks. Dave and I put our backs together like barroom brawlers waiting for an attack.

They were circling us. About the third time around I nudged Dave with my elbow and motioned with my thumb — up. We stayed back to back until we broke water next to the boat. The sharks had followed us to the surface.

Mike, seeing the sharks, ran to start the starboard engine. As soon as it fired, the sharks moved away.

Mike greeted us with a grin as we climbed aboard, which made Dave's face twist in a grimace. "Now we're in real trouble," he remarked. "All we're going to hear from now on is how Mike saved our lives."

Dave's sense of humor was still good, but my fanny and spirits were dragging. Now I was almost certain our galleon did not exist.

It was still early in the day and we continued to mag. When we reached 150 feet deep, I called a halt. Moving in toward shore, we anchored over the spot where we had found the coins. The next morning we re-magged the area close to shore. Still nothing.

Once more we anchored over the spot where we had luck, but this time to use our propwash blowers. In the next two days we cleaned out all the potholes and found twelve more coins. That was it.

When we decided there was nothing more in the water, Dave and I took the whaler ashore with the mag and started searching the beach. Again nothing. I knew our dream, which had been so promising just a few days earlier, was about to come to an end.

Dave and I began working with the metal detector once more, searching the sandy area inshore. I was operating the unit when I heard a loud hum. Yelling for Dave, he came running and together we dug. About two feet down we found rusty pieces of iron.

While I was trying to figure out what it was, Dave let out a yelp. He had found another piece of eight. Strangely, instead of being excited, it subdued us because we both realized that was the end of the Cayman Brac treasure.

It was quite clear what had happened. Someone in about 1700 had buried money in an iron chest about fifty feet inshore and for some reason was never able to return to retrieve his small hoard. Perhaps he was one of the pirates who had been killed at Bloody Bay. The time period is right.

In the years that followed the chest lay there deteriorating until the monstrous hurricane of 1932. As the giant waves crashed onshore, the sand protecting the chest was washed away. Another wave broke it open, spilling its contents. Wave after wave pounded in and scattered the coins across the beach carrying some into the water.

And that, unfortunately, was that!

12

THE STINGING VINE AND THE BENDS

HAULING ANCHOR THE NEXT MORNING, we sailed for Grand Cayman. It was the second week of April. The first of May we planned a trip with Bob Soto to Pedro Bank, about fifty miles southwest of Jamaica.

There are several wrecks on Pedro Bank, the shoals and reefs of which extend for almost 100 miles in an east-west direction. The bottom is irregular and it is extremely dangerous for navigation. But there is a wreck there worth going after, the Spanish galleon *Genovesa*, which sank in 1730. She was carrying millions in gold and silver when she went down, only part of which was salvaged.

Soto and his brother-in-law, Art McKee, thought they had located the wreck. They had recovered coins as well as a pile of artifacts.

Soto's boat, the *Cayman Pilot,* needed hauling and he did not have the necessary equipment to work a wreck. We did. So after conferring with McKee to be sure that he did not feel we would be jumping his claim, we decided to make the trip in May, historically a good-weather month.

We wanted to put the *Virg a Lona* in good condition for the 250-mile run. However, we figured we could do that in ten days or less. Which gave us another ten to search Grand Cayman's north coast and to check out a deep wreck an old fisherman claimed to have found.

On the second day back we were searching an area on the north end of the island that was all white sand on the bottom. The water was beautifully clear and even more beautifully calm.

Throughout the day we had run the mag over the area, then late in the afternoon I got a hit. Two more passes assured me there was something below.

85

After anchoring, I suited up, grabbed a spear gun, and headed for the bottom. There did not seem to be anything there. It seems strange to say this since the bottom was flat, but suddenly, out of nowhere, I came upon the solid wreckage of a two-masted schooner. The reason I had not seen it until I was almost on top of it was because the sand had built up a gradual mound that effectively hid the wreck from view in the direction from which I was swimming.

The anchor chain and gear from the ship were all in a pile. Poking about in the rubble I found some bottles about fifty years old. It was just another wreck, nice to look at but with nothing on it of real value.

I was about ready to head for the surface when I noticed a giant jewfish swimming at the entrance of a small cave in the reef about a hundred feet away. Easily it was a 200-pounder and would bring $40 at any of the resorts. It wasn't treasure but at the time $40 was $40.

Finning over to the reef, I watched the fish as it swam inside the cave. I hid at the entrance, but the fish would not come out. I peered into the hole. Nothing. Then I saw it, but just for a second. Again it was gone only to appear a minute later. It was tantalizing me.

Just as I was about to give up, the huge fish gave me a good shot at it. The spear plunged into its head just behind the right eye.

Reaching into the hole, I tried to get a grip on the six-foot spear. My fingertips just touched, yet I managed to pull it toward me just enough to get a hand on it.

As I slowly worked the fish towards the entrance, it became wedged in the rocks. Tugging did no good so I gave it a good yank, which had the effect of pulling me to the reef and not the fish to me.

Covering the reef was underwater vegetation that appeared to be a vine. My wet suit protected my body, but as I turned my head, my right ear came in contact with the vine. I felt a sharp pain and pulled away.

Rubbing my ear, the pain subsided. Then I went about the business of retrieving my fish. Because I had been working hard, I used my air more rapidly than usual. As I took a breath, I realized I was down to 300 pounds and pulled my reserve.

Finning along the bottom, I waited until I was directly under the *Virg a Lona* before pushing up. I was in forty feet of water. Halfway to the surface the pain in my ear became unbearable. I noticed as I stopped my ascent and slowly sank, my ear stopped hurting.

Again I started for the surface and again as I reached the halfway point, the pain became more than I thought I could bear. Sinking to the bottom, the pain again disappeared. I touched my ear. It had swollen to twice its normal size.

I stood on the bottom trying to figure my next move, not that I had many alternatives. In all my years of diving I had never encountered anything like this before. I was breathing my last from that tank, which helped me make a decision quickly.

Each breath became harder as I headed for the boat and I knew there was no more turning back. I left my $40 fish on the bottom so I had the use of both hands. Unhooking my weight belt, I carried it in my hand so if I passed out, I would instinctively drop it and continue to float to the surface.

At the halfway point I popped the CO_2 capsule on my safety vest to inflate it and that's the last I remember. I was unconscious when I broke water. Fortunately Mike and Dave had already started looking for me. Since the time I had been washed out to sea, we had all become more aware of how long a man was below.

Within seconds they had the *Virg a Lona* alongside, but lifting an unconscious man out of the water is extremely difficult and it was fifteen minutes before they had me aboard.

By the time I regained consciousness Dave had retrieved my fish, weight belt and spear gun. My ear hurt like hell, but aside from that I was all right.

After reaching shore, I visited the local doctor. He examined my ear and shook his head.

"I have no idea what caused the sting, nor do I have a cure for it," he said. "The sea contains a lot of hurts for which the medical profession has not yet discovered cures."

About the fourth day, my ear was back to normal and I forgot the incident. Eight months later, I boarded a plane in Miami for a flight to St. Louis. It was winter in the Midwest. As I stepped off the plane, a gust of icy air hit me. That fast my ear hurt so much I let out a yell. Almost instantly it became swollen. A day later the swelling subsided and I have never had trouble since.

The sea seemed intent on teaching me as much as it could in a short time. A week later I learned another painful lesson. Earlier I had mentioned I had met an old fisherman who claimed he could see the remains of an old wreck in very deep water. He had only been able to see it at certain times of the year when the water was flat and clear, but he said that there were cannons laying about.

Like so many of the island fishermen, he had spent much of his life looking into the sea through a glass-bottom bucket. It was people like him I had tried to contact when I first came to the island. It was worth checking out.

When I heard his story, he was confined to his bed so he was unable to personally show us the area. However, the description of the location was sufficient now that we were so familiar with the waters.

We were preparing for our trip with Bob Soto. After some minor repairs were made one morning, we headed out to sea so that we would be over the described wreck site when the sun was highest and we would have our best light.

After anchoring over what we figured to be the right spot, Dave and I suited up. We had already discussed what we would do. The plan was simple: We would dive, spread out and swim along the bottom, Dave on one side of the boat and I on the other. The shelf was sloping quickly here and Dave would be in deeper water than

I, perhaps he would be swimming at 120 feet. I would be in about 100 feet of water. Consequently, he would be coming up sooner.

We slipped into the water at the same time. The sun was high and hot so the water seemed refreshingly cool. We were only wearing our wet suit tops so it did not take too long before the refreshing cool became cold on our legs.

It was another world. No hurry, no noise, schools of tropical fish darting to get out of my way as I slowly worked my way to the bottom. I was caught up with just being there.

As I dove deeper, the only apparent activity was my air bubbles rushing to the surface. On the bottom I looked up to see the *Virg a Lona.* It seemed far away. I did not see Dave.

As I swam, I saw nothing at first. The visibility was good but considerably less than under the same light conditions in shallow water. I swam perhaps 300 feet when I came across the wreckage of a complete schooner, perhaps seventy-five years old.

Intact wooden masts were lying about. Apparently the vessel was deep enough to escape the ravages of the teredo worms. From the surface what the old man had seen were these masts. He had mistaken them for cannons.

I really did not expect much, so I was not disappointed. Yet it is always better to check out a story that seems to have some merit than to wonder and never know.

I was not used to deep diving and it seemed I had only been down a short time when I found it difficult to breathe. Looking at my watch, I was horrified to find that I had extended my bottom time by ten minutes.

When the next breath came even harder, I reached back and pulled my safety valve. Now the air flowed freely. I knew I had enough air to get to the top and as I ascended, I watched my air gauge.

There was not enough to make the usual decomprssion stop at forty feet so I continued up and stopped under the boat at ten feet until I exhausted my reserve. The bends passed through my mind as I was waiting, but I did not think I was down long enough at 100 feet to really be in trouble.

As I climbed aboard the *Virg a Lona,* Mike was waiting for me. He said Dave had been aboard about twenty minutes. He was below deck. Dave had never seen the wreck.

Unstrapping my equipment, I stowed it. Just as I finished, Dave came on deck.

"You sure were down a long time, man," he remarked. "Did you find anything?"

"A schooner," I replied. "About seventy-five years old. Hey Mike," I yelled. "Haul the anchor."

I was at the wheel as we headed in. Suddenly I felt as if I had a slight toothache in the lower part of my jaw. Within an hour everything in my mouth was hurting.

As we pulled into the dock, I became sick and vomited. I felt dizzy.

My equilibrium was gone and I fell backwards. I remember trying to get to my feet and that I was sweating profusely.

When I regained consciousness, I was in my bunk and Bob Soto was standing over me with his hand on my forehead.

"Can you move your arms and legs?" he asked.

I could.

"Roy," he said, gravely, "you're a lucky man."

I was, too, because there was no recompression chamber on the island. It was my only experience with the bends. Although I had a little difficulty in 1973 when Dick Richmond and I were down too long picking on the bones of the *Avisio* in Biscayne Bay in Florida. My jaw was sore for two days after that dive.

13
MAY HURRICANE

MY BOUT WITH THE BENDS was over more quickly than the episode a week earlier with the stinging vine, which had enlarged my ear so. By the time the first of May arrived, the *Virg a Lona* was ready for the trip to Pedro Bank.

This time we were determined to find treasure. Bob Soto had been there and had brought some back. No more slim pickings for us. In the year Dave and I had been in Cayman we had found a little here and a little there, but no strikes. We wanted a strike . . . **We needed one!** Time was always against us.

We were due to start May 2, but Bob had some unfinished business to attend to and we hauled anchor a day later than planned.

The weather was perfect, the sea calm as we pulled out of Georgetown and headed for East End. At East End we changed course and headed southeast on water that was almost like glass.

I stood alone on the bow for awhile breathing deeply, happy about my good fortune. Under me was a good boat, and with me were three good friends. On top of that we were heading for gold. I could smell it.

I thought that was what I was smelling. I think what I really got a whiff of was the hurricane that was moving in on us.

Living on the *Virg a Lona* as long as we had, we ignored her deficiencies. We had no automatic pilot, no loran nor any other fancy equipment. We had a ship-to-shore radio that worked most of the time, and a compass. However, someone once asked me if the compass had been part of a package deal. You know, Boy Scout uniform, jackknife, mess kit . . .

Because we had no automatic pilot we were standing the wheel in two-hour shifts. At about four in the afternoon I took over just as a wind started to kick up and the sky changed color.

It looked as if there was a rainstorm in the distance, but rainstorms were common and usually brief. At about 4:30 the sky was becoming dark and the wind was building. Now the *Virg a Lona* was getting a spray over her bow.

Bob Soto came up on deck and peered at the sky for a few moments. "It's going to blow up a storm," he said quietly. Bob was soft-spoken but his tone sounded ominous.

"Hurricane?"

"Too early. It'll pass over."

For the next hour things did not get any worse. Then the sky changed again — to an odd pink.

"Look at that!" I said to Bob.

"Yeah."

And then it hit. In minutes all hell broke loose. We could see the waves coming and then we were in them. Not on top, but right in the midst of waves twenty feet high.

Bob took the wheel. "We're in for it," he yelled.

Then all of a sudden the wind changed. It was coming from one direction and the waves another. The giant waves seemed to be standing still as we plowed through them.

Once more the wind shifted and I could hear the bones of the poor *Virg a Lona* creak as she was battered by the forces pounding and pulling at her, trying to rip her apart and crush her. Now the deficiencies that I had overlooked regarding the boat struck me.

I yelled to Bob, "Let's turn this damn thing around and get the wind at our stern."

"We can't," he yelled back. The noise was deafening as the waves crashed down on top of us and the wind was letting out a killer's scream. "If we turn and one of those waves hits us broadside, we'll turn over."

There was nothing we could do but run into the storm and hold on.

It was black, it was light. Black, light, black, light as the waves drowned us and we popped back. I had heard how howling can unnerve a man. I think the terror of that wind might have shaken me if I had not been staring in horrified fascination at the size of the waves engulfing us.

Then it came, the biggest wave I had ever seen in my life. It was so immense there was nothing else to see. It was going to waste us. Taking a deep breath, I held it and waited. The wave swooped down under the *Virg a Lona* and turned her completely around and dropped her. It sounded as if the hull had split open when we hit.

Now instead of driving into the wind, it was at our stern and with the big rollers behind us we were moving as if on a surfboard. The *Virg a Lona's* top speed was thirteen knots. We were doing thirty.

Bob set our course for Grand Cayman. "I don't think we'll make it," he said. "I doubt if this boat will hold together under this pounding."

Mike appeared relieved over our change in direction, but Dave had a sick look on his face.

"Don't worry," I assured him just as if I knew what I was talking about. "We'll make it OK."

"Don't you hear it?" he asked.

"Hear what?"

"Below deck."

I listened but didn't hear anything.

"She's full of water," Dave said. "The pumps can't handle it as fast as it's coming in."

When I opened the hatch, it looked like a swimming pool below. If we did not do something quickly, we were going to sink.

"Hook up the hale fire pump," I yelled.

"It doesn't work," Dave said. "You have to take it apart and play with it first."

"It better work or we're going under."

We hooked up the hoses and gave a yank on the starter. The motor fired the first try, and the water poured out of the hold. It did not get rid of it, but at least we were not taking on more than we could handle.

By the time the storm had hit we had run almost a hundred miles. We were back in Grand Cayman in less than half the traveling time. Once we saw the lights we ran around the island and got behind it for shelter.

We had a rough ride the rest of the night, but at daybreak we found the channel through the reef and made our way to calmer water.

No one could remember a hurricane hitting that early in May before. However, if Bob had not been delayed that one day we would have been out too far to turn back. We were alive. That was our good fortune. We might have found the *Genovesa* just in time to join it.

After the hurricane passed, Dave, Mike and I turned to getting the *Virg a Lona* in shape again. It was a mess, but in a week we had it looking pretty good.

I went to Bob Soto and asked if he would be interested in making another try for Pedro Bank.

"Roy," Bob said, looking me in the eye, "I don't want to chance another trip on the *Virg a Lona* like the one we just went through. She doesn't take big waves like an open-sea boat should. Five hundred miles out there all by herself is too much for her."

I nodded. He was right. The *Virg a Lona* had too much weight in the stern and was dead in the water. She was like a fighter who did not know how to ride with a punch.

"I'd take the *Cayman Pilot*," Bob said, "but she needs hauling. Besides she's not rigged out with a propwash."

Returning to the boat, Dave and I discussed the future. Our time in Cayman was coming to a close and we knew it. We washed and dressed, then went to the Beach Club for a turtle steak dinner.

When we arrived, there was a cable from Harold Still waiting for me. It had arrived that morning. It read, "Florida leases being issued next week." It was signed, "Harold."

Turning to Dave, I grinned, "Hell, here's our answer."

Both of us laughed and began patting each other on the back. Then it hit us: Mike. We could not take him with us because we could not guarantee him a job. Our funds were almost depleted and if we did not sell some of the coins we found, there was no way for the operation to last another six months.

When we returned to the boat, Dave would not look at Mike. Mike sensed something was wrong and he spoke my name. "What happened?" he asked.

"We're going back to the States."

Dave walked out on deck.

Mike said nothing. He just stared at me, tears welling up in his eyes. He knew I was going to tell him he would not be going with us before I told him why.

"You can't leave me, Roy."

"I have to. I can't pay you any longer."

"I'll work for nothing," he cried.

Shaking my head, I held out my hand. In it was two months wages. He took the money and we clasped hands. As he walked away, tears were rolling down his cheeks. I had to take a deep breath to keep from breaking up. Dave just stood with his back to me.

14

LONELY VOYAGE

IN THE NEXT TWO DAYS Dave and I prepared for the return voyage to Florida. We were loading a large compressor aboard the *Virg a Lona* when a wave hit the boat. Losing our footing, we stumbled and the compressor crashed against Dave and knocked him down.

He laid there shaking in pain. I tried to make him comfortable, then ran to call an ambulance. He was rushed to the hospital. After x-rays were taken, I was told that his shoulder had been damaged and that he would be all right. However, it would be several weeks before he could do any work. A boat trip to the States for him at this point was out of the question.

I told Dave the news about his shoulder. "You'll have to stay here, man," I said.

"What about you?"

"I'm going to get the *Virg a Lona* back to Florida."

"You can't do it alone," he protested.

"I cabled for help. Jack McBeth will be here tomorrow. When you get released, jump on a plane and I'll meet you in Miami. I've got to get back while the State is passing out leases or we may not get one."

Before we left Florida we had discovered several wrecks in the lower Keys. We had not worked them because our lease had been cancelled and we did not want to take a chance of working them illegally. We felt that once the new regulations were written there would be no reason for World Wide to be denied a lease.

The next day I bought Dave his return airline ticket and gave it to him along with a few hundred dollars to meet expenses until he could join me.

As I turned to leave, Dave said, "Roy, that damn boat won't make it. It's a floating death trap."

"I'll make it," I assured him. "I'm going to pick up Jack McBeth now."

McBeth was an old friend whose business it was to pilot boats from anyplace to anywhere. He knew more about navigation by instinct than most people can learn in a lifetime.

When Jack saw the *Virg a Lona,* he remarked, "I've had better boats than this sink under me. But if you're willing, I am."

I was willing and we cast off immediately. I watched the island until it faded from view. Dave and Mike were still there as well as John Cumber, Bob Soto and the scores of other friends I had made in my twelve months there. A man has nothing without good memories and that year had give me some of my best.

The sea was calm. Jack set a course for San Antonio Light at the western tip of Cuba. The two of us switched off at the wheel every four hours. The next afternoon we sighted Cuba and ran well out to sea along its coast.

About 3 p.m. Jack spotted a vessel headed in our direction at high speed. As it came closer, we could tell it was a patrol boat and I ran up an American flag.

Jack radioed the United States Coast Guard at Key West and reached the operator. He gave the operator our position.

"We're at least twenty-five miles off the coast of Cuba," he reported, then stepped out on deck so that the Cubans could see him on the radiophone. "We have visitors. A Cuban patrol boat is keeping us company and I just wanted you to know."

The Cubans ran alongside for about five minutes then veered off toward shore. Shortly the patrol boat was out of sight.

At San Antonio Light Jack reset our course. I could not sleep so I told Jack to get some shut-eye and I would wake him when I became tired.

As soon as we rounded the Light, I found a storm. The wind kicked up and waves started slapping us around. What was worse was that it was so dark that I could not see a thing.

It was another test for the nerves but I stayed at the wheel until dawn, then Jack took over as I tried to sleep. However, the storm seemed to get worse and I was hard-pressed not to roll out of my bunk. My main concern was that the *Virg a Lona* was holding together. She seemed to be.

That night we pulled into Key West and docked at a pier. Then both of us got some needed rest. The next morning while we were waiting for the Customs officer to check us in, we took on fuel and decided to pump the boat. Both pumps were out and probably had been for most of the voyage.

Jack looked below. "My Lord!" he exclaimed and whistled softly. "If we had been hit by a big storm, we probably wouldn't have made it."

I looked, too, but "My Lord" is not what I said.

After clearing Customs, I purchased two battery-operated pumps and we set sail again, this time for Key Largo. That night I was at the wheel and I guess I really did not know how tired I actually was.

As we were running up Hawk's Channel, the water was smooth, so smooth I began to grow sleepy, partly out of monotony, partly because I was bushed. Nearing Key Largo, I saw what I mistook for channel marker lights. Suddenly the water became rough. Waves began to crash against our bow. I stepped out of the cabin. There was no wind. Why the waves? Then I realized what I had done. I had moved out of the channel and into the shipping lanes. I was again riding the wake of a huge freighter. The lights I had seen were ship lights.

Moving back into the channel, I anchored and went to sleep. The next morning, as we pulled in to dock, Jack's wife, who had driven down from Miami to pick him up, was there waiting for him. After paying Jack his fee, I thanked him and said goodby.

Harold Still drove down the next day. He looked great for a 9-to-5 family man who was selling insurance. But underneath that businessman exterior, I could see the treasure hunter yet inside him.

He handed me a newspaper that explained the new treasure-hunting regulations. Another article listed the companies that had been issued leases. World Wide was not among them.

This hit me harder than anything that had happened in all my time at Cayman. I called Robert Williams, a former state senator who was employed as the director of the Board of History and Archives in Tallahassee.

I was told that only companies best qualified to do the job were granted leases. I looked over the list. Some of the outfits not only knew nothing about treasure hunting, they did not even own a boat.

"Politics," I said to myself. "Rotten politics."

I felt as if I had reached the end of the rainbow and someone had beaten me to the pot.

15

SILVER BY THE BUCKETFULS

NO GOLD.
No nothing.

Everything I had refused to see had become perfectly clear in that hard moment of truth. I knew Dave Meinell had been offered a good job in St. Louis. He was going to take it, I was sure. Harold, when he handed me that newspaper, had been sad because he knew it was over, too. In reality it had been over for him for a year. Art Hartman was now working with Mel Fisher and Treasure Salvors and was doing very well.

Harold and I had discussed the possibility of searching for the *Maravillas* in the Bahamas. I told him some of my conclusions and he agreed that Orellana's galleon had to be either at Red Riding Rocks or on Little Bahama Bank. Yet only a year had passed and the Bahamian government still wasn't much interested in talking to treasure hunters. "Only a year," I said aloud. So much had happened in those twelve months it seems incredible so little time had passed.

When Harold walked away, I knew I was alone, and I did not want to be. I flew home to be with my wife and children.

After several days of hiding away, I contacted the shareholders in World Wide and called a meeting. The facts were clear regarding the men and the lease.

"On top of that," I reported, "the *Virg a Lona* needs an overhaul. Our mag is malfunctioning and needs work. We still have some money, but not enough to tackle any major project. I think we should sell the boat, liquidate our equipment and dispose of the treasure and artifacts we do have. Let's call it an experience."

Everyone agreed and I was asked to return to Florida and liquidate everything. School had just closed for the summer so the family piled into the car and we headed south.

At Key Largo, I rented an apartment and set about the task of unloading everything World Wide owned. Airlifts, dredges, compressors and all the equipment needed for what we had been doing had cost plenty to build or buy, but there was no market for them when it came to selling. Only other treasure hunters wanted what I was trying to unload and they did not have any money.

In the several weeks it took to dispose of the equipment, my apartment became the meeting place for treasure hunters throughout the Keys. It was then that Art McKee, the granddaddy of all Florida treasure hunters, and I became friends. He knew more about shipwrecks and artifacts than anyone I had ever met and could tell a story with such alacrity I learned almost as much just bumming around with him as I had by experience. It was he who told me years later that I had become the legend of the Caymans. When I had sailed away from Georgetown, I had done so the day after Dave had been injured.

The story had it that we had found a lot of treasure and I had tried to kill him to keep from sharing it with him. A stranger had arrived immediately thereafter and when we left, we had so much treasure aboard that the *Virg a Lona* was low in the water. I laughed over what Art was saying, but later I wondered just how many other treasure stories had started the same way.

Art McKee was an old hard-hat diver who had been picking on wrecks in the Keys since 1937. Fifteen minutes in a swimming pool and he became a scuba diver. He took to it so easily he made some of us experienced scuba divers look a little retarded.

One thing about having crazy treasure hunters around; it made Margie, my wife, realize I was not the only one. There were lots like me who had gold fever.

Finally, I was able to sell all the equipment, but I was still stuck with a treasure-hunting boat that needed an overhaul. I tried everything I knew to sell the *Virg a Lona*, but short of almost having to give her away I could not seem to put together a deal.

While waiting for two interested parties to give me the nod, I grew restless. Then one morning an old acquaintance, whom I'll call Sammy for reasons that will become clear later, came to the apartment and asked me if I would like to join him in looking for one of the treasure galleons of the 1622 fleet.*

Fifteen months earlier Harold Still, Dave Meinell, Bill Filer and I had spent four weeks searching the water off Matacumbe Key for the *Margarita* and *Nuestra Senora de Atocha*. It was a fruitless search, but I listened to what Sammy had to say.

He had found a large anchor in sixty feet of water, which looked to be of the right period. He said he would furnish the boat if I would furnish the fuel. Anything we found would be split on a fifty-fifty

*See Chapter 5 — INTO TREASURE HUNTING FEET FIRST — FLAT FEATS.

basis.

I agreed to work with him only until I could sell the *Virg a Lona.* I had known this treasure hunter some time, but not too well. However, I figured I had little to lose. With the kind of luck I had been having, maybe it would change through him.

Sammy was a scrounger. He wasted nothing. If we found a wreck with nothing of apparent value, he would pick up the brass spikes and sell them for scrap. Yet he would work long hours. Seldom did we come in before dark. This part about Sammy I liked.

However, there was another side of Sammy, the part that disturbed me. It seemed that Sammy had had trouble with just about every treasure hunter with whom he had worked. It set me to wondering. I knew a few of his former partners and they all seemed to be pretty good guys. Yet Sammy did not have a good word for any of them. Then, too, Sammy seemed to have an intense fear of sharks and barracuda. It made me think he might leave me below if things got tight.

Our search methods were simple. Primitive is probably a better word. We would take turns dragging each other behind the boat as we looked through our face masks and breathed through our snorkels.

The bottom was mostly flat and it was easy to spot formations that did not look exactly the way they should. In the area in which we were searching, there was little sand and little the hardpan could conceal. In three weeks we did not find a treasure wreck, but we covered a lot of territory.

Late one evening, when I arrived home, Art Hartman was there waiting for me. Both of us had changed. We had become lean and hard. I was bronzed from the sun; Art's hair was much longer and sun-bleached blond. We looked the part of what we now were and each of us laughed about it. It was good seeing him, really good, because in spite of what had happened I knew we both had clung to the friendship that had started us on this path.

Art had driven down from Fort Pierce to inform me that Mel Fisher's work boat had fallen apart.

"Fisher," he said, "is interested in buying the *Virg a Lona.*

"With half a good diving season still in front of him, he needs a boat and fast."

I phoned Mel and he drove down the next night. He looked the *Virg a Lona* over as soon as he arrived. I told him the boat needed work, but he could see that.

"The engines need work, too," I told him.

"Sail her to Fort Pierce tomorrow," he said. "It'll take a week or so to get her into shape, but she's rigged out pretty good with blowers and all. What's a few days off."

It was a typical Fisher snap decision. There was no haggling or kicking the boat to see if it would go flat. Fisher knew what he was buying and he was willing to pay a fair price for it. Not that he was the least bit foolish; he quickly sized up things and situations, then moved. It was this that made him one of the leading treasure finders in the world, and why many of the same people stuck with him for years.

The deal was made and Art sailed the boat to Fort Pierce. I would follow in a couple of days with Margie and the kids.

Traveling north on U.S. 1 from the Keys, I could see in Margie's eyes that this fast-moving life was nothing she wanted to get used to. Until I became involved in treasure hunting, she had had a 9-to-5 husband and all the normal family activities built around home and children.

I decided as soon as the deal was consumated, I would return to St. Louis and get back into a routine. I had seen more than one person stricken with gold fever become distant from his family and I didn't feel any treasure was worth that.

When I had the family settled in a motel in Vero Beach, I promised Margie I was through with all this crazy treasure diving.

"Just as soon as I've settled the boat deal with Mel Fisher," I vowed, "we're heading home. I'll be a 9-to-5 man again."

Margie could not have been happier.

The next day the papers were signed and the *Virg a Lona* was Mel's. That night Margie and I were invited to Mel's house for a party. I mentioned Mel's business sense. As a personality, he is flamboyant and friendly, the kind of person who creates an atmosphere of golden opportunities with every man to whom he talks. He had made his fantasies of treasure come true and so everyone who shares the same fantasies listens. The great or the terrible thing about this ability to create an atmosphere, depending upon your point of view, is a person can see his own dreams being realized as Mel talks.

At one point during the evening, Mel cornered me and we started talking treasure, then he broke out some of the finds he had kept at home. I was about to take part in salvaging the greatest treasure find in history, only I didn't know it yet.

Into my hands he poured a half dozen gold escudos in mint condition, and perfect silver coins. I can't describe the feeling that comes over you when you touch gold. It was there and I was holding it, but it was not mine.

The gold fever had me again and when Mel suggested I stay on in Vero Beach and join him and his company for the rest of the diving season, I listened. My promise to Margie was forgotten.

My percentage would be small, but I saw a chance to make some money. I also knew the people in Mel's outfit were first class in treasure hunting. I would learn. I wanted to know more about magnetometers, about obtaining research, about different ways of using blowers. There was so much to know and I felt I knew so little.

I did not say yes immediately, but told Mel I would let him know the next day. I wanted to talk to Margie first. When I told her of Mel's offer, she replied, "Do what you think best."

From her tone I knew she was far from excited about it. I tossed and turned that night and got very little sleep. When I awakened the next morning, Margie said, "If you want, I'll look around for an apartment today."

That was all the answer I needed. As usual, she let me have my way. I felt like an ass, but only until Mel arrived and started talking about the pile of gold we would find that day.

I believed him, but as it turned out, we were unable to go out that day or the several that followed. The weather had turned rough. Our first full day out was exciting to me as we anchored over the wreck

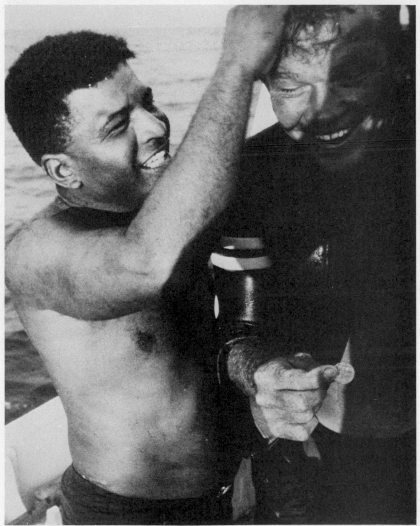

Demostines Molinar (left) congratulates Roy Volker after Volker found his first gold coin after joining Mel Fisher's Treasure Salvors in 1966. Treasure Salvors was working on the Colored Beach wreck at the time.

Volker (left), Mel Fisher (center) and Kip Wagner with the silver-coin-covered anchor of the 1715 ship off the Cabin Beach wreck at Sebastian Inlet, Florida.

south of Fort Pierce off Colored Beach. With the first hole we blew I went over the side and came up with a handful of silver pieces of eight.

Mel and his group stood on deck leaning over the rail waiting for me to surface. They laughed like crazy when they saw how excited I was. It was old hat to them, but to me . . .

The only things that really caused a stir with them was gold or an unusual artifact. This Gold Wreck was a strange one because it produced so few artifacts.

One day I found a bucketful of silver coins, a gold two escudo and a small buckle. When I surfaced with my finds, everyone showed more interest in the buckle than they did in the gold and silver.

Besides Mel and his wife, Delores, there were his partners, Fay Field, Dick Williams, Rupert Gates, Walt Holzworth and Demostines Molinar. It was a good association from the start. Within a short time I felt like one of them and I loved it.

I was a diving treasure hunter who was on a wreck that seldom produced an empty hole. The satisfaction was almost overwhelming.

Mel's Treasure Salvors at the time had a working contract with the Real Eight Corporation, which was then headed by Kip Wagner. Real Eight's leases stretched for about forty-five miles from Sebastian Inlet south to Jupiter Inlet. In its lease area were the wrecks of the ten ships of the plate fleet that sank on July 31, 1715, in a hurricane. Not all the ships have yet been found, including the capitana of the fleet, the main treasure ship. The Spanish themselves salvaged many of the wrecks. However, with the methods then available their efforts were limited.

Kip Wagner's outfit had a gold-producing wreck at Cabin Beach right at Sebastian Inlet and that is where his group spent most of its time. Eventually that wreck produced treasure worth millions of dollars and made Kip a rich man.

The two groups worked in co-operation, yet there was a spirit of friendly rivalry between them. More than once we would participate in coin-finding contests. On one day just as we were clearing the Indian River inlet to work our wreck, Mel altered course.

"We need a change of scenery," he announced. "Let's go dig with Kip and his boys on the Cabin Wreck."

Mel was a hunch player whose hunches paid off too frequently for anyone to offer an argument. Running up the coast, we pulled into shore about a hundred feet from Kip's boat, which was digging at the time.

Kip yelled a greeting and Mel called back. There were a few things said, then suddenly we were in a contest for a case of beer. The way we went at it one would have thought that the crown jewels were at stake. We did not even stop for lunch.

Kip's boat was tied to the ring of an old giant anchor from the wreck, which made Mel grumble. He usually used that anchor when

Delores Fisher brings up in 1966 a pewter plate from one of the 1715 wrecks. Behind her is her husband, Mel. *(Roy Volker Photo)*

we worked the site. Not that there was much left of the original. The flukes were broken off and about all that was left was the large ring and the long shank. However, it did provide good mooring and Mel grumbled even more when we had trouble setting our own anchors.

Finally we managed to settle down to blowing holes. Although we were working as if there was no tomorrow, little treasure was brought up that day. Our group had collected only about 100 pieces of eight for its efforts; Kip's group had half that. It looked as if the beer would be ours.

Then I noticed Kip's crew straining to pull something aboard its boat. We did not know what until we returned to the dock. Mel went to see what had caused that last-minute surge of manpower.

What Kip and company had pulled aboard was the shank and anchor ring that Mel had been using for mooring for all those months. On the end of the shank opposite the ring was a mass of coins that had fused together and to the shank in those hundreds of years in the sea.

Everyone laughed over the incident, but I think Kip enjoyed it the most. He had the coins and the beer.

Often one never knows what he is looking at underwater. A similar incident happened to Walt Holzworth, one of Mel's group. He was using a metal detector, working the bottom around the wreck south of Fort Pierce.

Walt had weighted himself down enough so he could walk around on the bottom and use his detector as a coin shooter might who was used to working on land. He was a water hog and could stay down most of the day with a hookah, and that day the water was clear and the surge was small.

He was having some success so he was reluctant to come to the surface even when he grew tired. Instead he found a mound on the bottom and sat for a time. After a short rest, he turned his metal detector on and bang, right where he had been sitting he got a big reading.

Removing the sand, he found a clump containing several hundred coins. It demonstrates how close a person can be to treasure and almost miss it.

Crystal water at Fort Pierce is unusual. Most of the time the water is murky and not the best for diving for more reasons than one. The obvious one is a diver has to work with his nose pretty close to the bottom to see; the other is sharks.

Kip Wagner noted in his book "Pieces of Eight" that the sharks seemed to remember a great feast day in 1715 and never left. More than a thousand persons lost their lives in that tragedy.

The water is murky at the site of the Colored Beach wreck because there is no barrier reef to break up the surge of waves coming in toward shore. The constant rolling action stirs up the sand and carries it into the beach with the surf. The undertow sucks it back.

Only when the ocean has been dead calm for several days does the water clear. Needless to say this almost never happens.

A 1711 specimen from a clump of silver coins found by Roy Volker in 1966, on a wreck near Vero Beach, Florida.
(Dick Richmond Photo)

Roy Volker (right), the season-ed professional treasure hunter, and Lloyd Bridges, the actor known for his association with diving from his television pro-gram, "Sea Hunt," and others.

When I had been working with Treasure Salvors for about three weeks, late one afternoon I jumped into the water to check a hole that had just been blown out. Hardly had I reached bottom than I spotted coins scattered all over the area.

After picking up the silver pieces of eight at the bottom of the hole, I began to fan the crevices in the bedrock with my glove hand for more when I felt something against my right shoulder. Turning my head, I found myself staring at the side of a shark so large I could see neither the head nor the tail.

As it moved slowly past, its long body rubbed against mine. A chill shot through me and I froze as a deer hunter who just spotted a stag. I was not being calm; I was too scared to move.

It took that monster five seconds, perhaps ten, to pass. It seemed more like ten minutes. Just as the shark's tail was rubbing against my back, someone topside gave a short blast on the blower and the shark sped away, knocking off my face mask with a flip of its tail.

The blast was a signal to clear out, another hole was about to be blown. I didn't bother to look for my mask. I sped to the surface and climbed aboard to find some place to sit and be sick.

When I told the others what had happened, no one made any jokes. Each and every one of them had had similar experiences.

Years later when Art Hartman was in charge of diving operations for Doubloon Salvage, Dick Richmond and I joined him for a week after we had returned from an expedition to the Bahamas. Dick was in these waters alone when he suddenly found himself swimming with a twelve-foot hammerhead. When he climbed aboard, he did not say much, but he didn't dive the rest of the day.

I know the feeling well. For the next week after that experience of mine I found myself looking over my shoulder whenever I was in the water.

August finally arrived and I had to put Margie and the children on a train for St. Louis. It seemed as if I was always saying goodby to them and my emotions showed. There were tears enough for everyone that day.

However, I felt I would be seeing them soon. Usually the water around Fort Pierce became so rough in September that from then until May no work was done on the wrecks. When the work stopped at Colored Beach, I promised Art Hartman I would travel to the Keys and help him dig out a wreck we had found almost two years earlier.

16
NOUVEAU RICHÉ FOR A DAY

MARGIE NO SOONER LEFT than the weather became rough. It was not so bad we could not work, yet it was an indicator the season was about over. When a storm blew in three weeks later, I told Mel Fisher I would be heading south for a couple of weeks to work a wreck with Art, but would drive back to see him before leaving Florida. Mel paid me off and wished me luck.

The following day I was in Marathon, where Art had set up a machine shop and a dive shop. It took us several days to get the boat in shape to work the wreck. The wreck was a mystery to us. We had no idea what it was.

The ballast pile did not seem large enough for the ship to have been a galleon, yet the stones were themselves so large that it would have been unlikely for them to be in a ship smaller than a galleon.

The wreck was old. This we surmised by the iron spikes we had found on it. From the few pieces of broken Chinese porcelain we had found, we guessed it to be a Spanish wreck.

One morning when we were finally ready, Art and I sailed out toward Duck Key. A lot had happened to both of us in those years since he had taken me on my first lake dive and I had quit after a minute because I wound up with my head in the mud.

Perhaps we had matured, perhaps the multiple disappointments had made us realize that only with a tremendous amount of luck could a man get rich quick in treasure hunting. We both knew it was possible to make a lot of money with a constant day-in, day-out effort . . . but was it really worth it? All the work, all the problems, the incredible dangers; anyone listening would have thought we were ready to turn around and head back for Marathon.

Then there we were on top of our wreck and the bad-mouthing

we had just been giving treasure hunting was forgotten. The storm had not yet hit the Keys and the water where we would be diving was clear and calm.

Casting an anchor, we let the current drift the boat over the ballast pile, which was scattered over the bottom. Once the boat was tied off, we threw the airlift over the side and fired up the compressor motor.

The wreck was in thirty-five feet of water and the bottom was sandy. We started the airlifting operation near a small grass patch and within minutes found cannon balls, grape shot and more pieces of Chinese porcelain.

It was more than four hours before we found our first coin, which was a badly corroded piece of eight. The coin was not dated, but we could tell that it had been minted in Mexico City during the reign of Philip V of Spain, which put it somewhere between 1700 and 1746. That did not mean our wreck was from that period; it just let us know that it was not any earlier than that.

After lunch Art and I headed for the bottom again. This time, instead of working in a single area, we started bouncing around with the airlift, digging holes all around the ballast pile. I found a medallion and Art found a badly oxidized cross. It was not much, but it was encouraging. At least we were beginning to think the wreck really was Spanish.

That night we anchored at Duck Key. We did not mind that the first day had brought us so little; the next day promised more. More than we expected. At 2 a.m. we were hit by a storm and we spent most of the night tying everything down. Even at dockside the boat was bouncing.

During the night, the wind kicked up to 30 miles an hour. At dawn, it was still howling and the rain, which had blown in with the wind, was getting worse. Small craft warnings were out.

I took the only option open to me: I cussed.

Art laughed and remarked, "So you want to be a treasure hunter, do you?"

I had to laugh, too.

The weather was not much better the following day, but the wind had calmed enough for us to head up the channel for Marathon, where Art's wife, Shirley, greeted us with a home-cooked meal.

It was ten days before we could return to Duck Key and our mystery wreck. The weather was pretty good and we managed to stay out three days before having to return for supplies. In those three days Art had found two more coins, a pewter plate and what was left of a fork.

We both were beginning to think while the wreck did have some potential, it was definitely not a treasure wreck.

"You want to pull off?" I asked Art.

Art shook his head. "Let's keep on it for two more days," he said, "and if we don't hit any more than we have, I'll take you to a wreck on which I've been finding some coins. Maybe that one will produce

Art Hartman (right), and Roy Volker in August 1966 with the coins and artifacts they found on an undetermined wreck of the 1733 fleet that sank in the Florida Keys.

more than we're finding here.''

The next day went by with our finding the usual trash. However, on the final day we had allowed ourselves, we had not been in the water more than an hour when we started uncovering coins two and three at a time.

Working in a circular area no larger than fifteen feet in diameter, we found coin after coin all through the day. Only nightfall forced us to the surface. Both of us were all smiles as we sat at the table below deck counting and sorting the silver. Altogether we found 196 coins in denominations of four and eight reals that day. The ship was from the fleet that sank in 1733, of that we were now reasonably certain.

The next morning we were over the side and on the bottom at 7. We returned to our hot spot, which seemed to have cooled during the night. That day's digging produced five coins and what we thought was an eight-pound hunk of lead. The hunk of lead turned out to be silver.

The next two days produced nothing. Art figured the wreck had been salvaged before and we had hit it lucky in finding those coins. We pulled anchor and headed for Marathon.

At dockside we were greeted by a few of Art's friends, to whom we showed our find. By the time we arrived at Art's home, there was a reporter there from the Keynoter newspaper. The Thursday, September 1, 1966, edition of the Keynoter carried our story and picture on the front page.

The wreck was outside the three-mile limit. That did not change until Tom Gurr found the *San Jose* in 1968. The State could not claim any part of the find and we figured we had cleaned the wreck out so we did not care who knew. What we did not know was the Associated Press had picked up the story and had blown it way out of proportion.

The next day we were getting phone calls from across the country from people who wanted to buy coins, others who wanted to buy part of our action. Everyone who was not buying was selling something. Being nouveau riché for a time was fun.

What was better was being with Art again and making a find with him. The treasure hunt had been Bill Settlemoir's idea, but it had been Art who had been the driving force that had gotten World Wide moving.

After he left I would hear from him now and again, but not often. He was still struggling to make a go of it in 1966 when we hit that pocket of coins at Duck Key, but he would have many of his own adventures and for three seasons take over the diving operation of Doubloon Salvage.

17
IN A SEA OF POISONOUS SNAKES

WHEN I BID FAREWELL TO ART at Marathon after our find on the 1733 ship in August 1966, I drove to Fort Pierce to pick up some of my gear. I had a wife and children who needed me and I was going home.

I was wondering if I was ever going to kick that damn gold fever as I was unloading a box off the *Virg a Lona*. Just as I lifted it from the deck to the dock, I felt something pop in my lower back.

There are ways to describe pain, but I am not sure I can do it justice in this case. All I can say is it was almost a week before I could sit in a car to drive.

Under the best of circumstances in those days, driving from Fort Pierce to St. Louis was tiring. This was before the days of the interstate highways. The trip was excruciating and it took me twice as long as it normally would have. After a time the pain grew bearable, but eventually I would have to have an operation.

Being from the Midwest a person does not realize how much he misses autumn until he has not experienced it for a time. I remember the exhilaration of my first autumn after being in the South Pacific in World War II. This time I arrived home as the leaves were turning red and yellow and gold. A cold snap had made the weather brisk. I loved it.

For the first time in almost two years I would be living in a comfortable house, eating home-cooked meals and having my wife and children around me.

I think my return would have been perfect if my back had not been hurting so much. I knew I would be heading for the hospital soon and that would cost a bundle. Money in those days was something of which I was uncomfortably short. I had some treasure and a pile of

111

artifacts, but it is difficult to exchange them for groceries. The pieces of eight would have to be sold, but in the meantime I needed a job.

One of the backers of World Wide Treasure Research was a phonograph record distributor and I stopped to see him to discuss what had happened since we were together last. Before I left I was hired as his promotion manager.

The money was not much but it paid the bills. At the time I was more interested in hospitalization than in getting rich. Pain limits one's thinking to pain.

Margie was pleased and so was I, for a time. After several months of being a white collar worker, I grew restless again. Just about the time I was feeling the pinch of city life, I received a call from Sammy, the treasure hunter with whom I had worked in search of the 1622 galleons in the Florida Keys.

It was February 1967 and Sammy had just returned from Ecuador. He had with him some gold and silver coins and said it looked as if he was onto something big.

Sammy needed backing and someone with a magnetometer. I agreed to discuss his propositon with the World Wide stockholders.

The equipment had been liquidated but the corporation had not as yet been formally dissolved. There was still some money in the kitty . . . not much . . . yet enough for the kind of project I guessed Sammy had in mind.

The stockholders were interested in hearing what he had to say. A few weeks later Sammy flew to St. Louis for a meeting to explain what he had found and what he wanted.

"I was at a sports show in Miami trying to unload some of my coins," he said, "when I was approached by an old man and an old woman. They said they had found similar coins on a beach in Ecuador where they had lived as children.

"I was invited to their home to see the coins. I was shown three Spanish gold escudos and four silver pieces of eight. I noticed each of the coins showed signs of water wear."

Sammy grew excited as he related the story and was beginning to gesture vigorously with his hands.

"The old couple wanted nothing from me," he insisted. "They did not try to sell me the coins. They had no motive for lying."

"I've been a patsy before," Sammy admitted, "so just to be sure I visited the old couple again. I asked them the same questions in different ways, trying to trick them into changing their story. It was always the same. The coins were always found on shore after storms.

"I knew I was onto something and I had a decision to make. I could invest the little money I had on a trip to Ecuador to check out the story first-hand, or I could forget the whole thing.

"I went," he said, then unfolded a piece of black velvet he had been carrying in his coat pocket. On the velvet were four gold coins and a half dozen silver ones. "I found these with a metal detector on the beach the old couple had described to me.

"I tried to do some diving," he told us, "but the surf was too heavy."

I looked at the coins. The earliest was minted in 1697, the latest in 1700. Each one showed water wear.

"I found them scattered across the beach," Sammy said. "They couldn't have come from a cache."

I remembered the Cayman Brac treasure. That, too, had been found scattered across the beach, but that treasure had come from a cache. There was one real difference between the two money beaches. The coins that Dave Meinell and I had found on land at Cayman Brac did not show the water wear of those that Sammy was showing us.

"I think what we have here," Sammy said, "is a ship offshore. The ship probably was carrying a consignment of coinage from the various South American mints to Panama where it would be shipped overland by mule to Porto Bello, and then on to Spain aboard another ship.

"For some reason the ship ran aground and broke up off this beach either in a storm or by navigational error."

Everyone looked at me.

"Could be," I said. "When were the coins first discovered?"

"In 1932," he replied. "The area was hit by a devastating hurricane and tidal wave. After it was over, people were finding gold and silver coins all over the beach."

What a remarkable coincidence! I thought. A hurricane the same year as the one that hit Cayman Brac!

Sammy's deal was simple. He would split everything found on a fifty-fifty basis for backing, and for a man to return to Ecuador with him.

"The man will have to be a diver," he said, "and have experience in operating a workable mag. I have to know the mag is all right or it's no deal."

Sammy was told we would discuss his proposition and let him know within a few weeks. When I drove him back to the airport, I said, "Look, man, I think there's a good chance my people will go for it, but there's no way in the world I'm going to be the guy who represents World Wide on this trip. My back is killing me."

Sammy nodded and we discussed the possibility of one of the others going.

The World Wide stockholders decided to take a gamble. With a working mag, they figured Sammy's theory could be proven or disproven quickly. The only problem was our mag did not work, and sending it back to the manufacturer was out of the question.

My neighbor, John Kowalski, who had been helping me with electronic problems for a number of years, was our only hope. I told him what the mag seemed to be doing, or not doing.

He said, "Leave it for a week. I'll see what I can do."

A week later I stopped by and he had it ready. By trial and error he had repaired a multitude of problems, and had even designed a different type of sensing head, one that proved to be far superior to the one that had come from the factory. I was impressed because I knew John was a tinkerer and not a trained electronics man.

Sammy was contacted and he insisted on a demonstration under conditions similar to those in Ecuador, meaning a salt water trial. I was selected to fly to Miami for a weekend to put the mag through its trials. It performed better than it ever had before.

Before leaving Miami, I set up a final meeting with the World Wide stockholders and Sammy in St. Louis. I furnished him with an airline ticket for the following week.

At the meeting Sammy refused to accept the person chosen to accompany him.

"His diving experience is too limited," he said. "I want Volker."

"I can't. My back hurts."

However, Sammy's timing was perfect. He had the World Wide people licking their chops and he set me up. The man for whom I worked pleaded with me to go.

"OK," I said, reluctantly.

My back obviously was not my only problem now. How was I going to explain Ecuador to Margie? I might be gone several months. She pretended she understood, but I know she didn't.

I was learning about Sammy, but there was a lot more to know. I was in Miami the following month, helping to crate the equipment we would need for the trip.

"I think we ought to take a third diver," he suggested.

"What?!"

"We may need someone. It will take the diving load off us."

"A third diver was not part of the deal," I countered. "Who did you have in mind?" I was willing to listen because I remembered Sammy's reaction to sharks and barracuda. Figuring if those South American waters were as infested with sharks as I guessed them to be, I would be the one who would be doing all the diving. As it turned out, it was more than a sea full of sharks I had to worry about, but the next lesson was still to come.

"A kid," Sammy said in response to my question. "His name is Tory Dowsett."

Tory was eager and friendly. He had plenty of diving experience. I liked him right away.

"OK," I said. "I'll pay his expenses and if anything is found he'll get a percentage or a bonus."

Sammy was elated to have me paying Tory's expenses, but was reluctant to spell out a given percentage for him ahead of time. I thought that strange. I always set percentages before a trip so that there would be no misunderstandings later.

"We're going to have to pick up some snake antivenin," Sammy said.

"What!" I said with less surprise than I felt.

"Sea snakes," he said. "Place is loaded with them."

I remembered discussing sea snakes with Ben Cropp of Australia once. He told me that there was no known antidote for the venom.

"You didn't say anything about sea snakes in St. Louis," I complained.

"I must've forgot."

I began to wonder what other little facts he had forgotten to mention. I will be the first to admit snakes give me the creeps, but I figured if Sammy would dive in those waters then surely I would.

There may not be a known antidote for sea snake venom, but I purchased $100 worth of antivenin regardless. The experts might be wrong.

"I need a new wet suit," Sammy said. "Your company agreed to pay for the equipment needed for the trip."

We bought him a new wet suit.

A picture was beginning to form — in panoramic vision — and I didn't like what I was seeing. The scrounger was scrounging with my company's funds.

"You know," he said, "we'll be using our own metal detectors while in Ecuador. Since they'll probably take a beating, I think World Wide ought to buy ours."

"No," I snapped. Recalling the moment, I don't think "no" was the word I used, but Sammy got the idea.

Once he realized the shopping spree was over, that no more surprises were in order, we boarded a plane for Panama. From Panama we flew to Guayaquil, Ecuador, where we rented a truck and headed for the coast and a small town called Salinas.

The countryside would not inspire a poet. In fact, the most interesting part of the two-hour trip were the roadblocks we encountered. Soldiers with fixed bayonets were looking for Communist terrorists who had gunned down a local bank president.

The soldiers and numerous dead donkeys along the road made the trip notable. It seemed no one there took care of their animals. They were allowed to roam freely. Although this was bad for the domestic animal population, it kept the buzzards full. Not much was tended to from what I could see, but then nothing was wasted either.

At Salinas we purchased two twelve-volt batteries for the magnetometer. From there we proceeded to Punta Canero. There were oil rigs all over the place. It struck me as it must have others that I was in a land in which I witnessed only people who were incredibly poor and yet the land was obviously rich in mineral wealth.

Eventually the road ran parallel to the Pacific. I could see the surf was heavy. Huge waves were crashing against the shore, bringing with them dingy looking water. Taking a break, we stopped at a fishing village and watched boats being unloaded. The catch was sharks, piles of them, sorted according to size — hammerheads, blues, browns, white tips and makos.

There were hundreds of them and seeing so many made us look at one another. Sammy kind of half grinned. Tory shrugged. I could feel my return airline ticket burning a hole in my pocket. Never had I wanted to use something so much in my life.

The sharks, which ranged in length from twenty-footers to three-footers, were caught for their hides, liver and fins. The fins were put through a drying process, ground into powder and sold as an aphrodisiac in Asia.

As we walked through the village, Tory and I noticed that Sammy seemed to be in deep thought. At the dock there were several boats tied up and I was looking them over when I noticed a boy about ten hand-line fishing.

I watched the boy as he lowered his line into the dirty water and pulled out a small fish. A moment later he had another bite. When he pulled it out of the water, I yelled. My Spanish is lousy, but somehow I got the point across the scorpion fish he had hooked was poisonous.

Tory and I looked at each other. What else? I thought.

We continued on to the resort at Punta Canero where we had planned to live during our stay in Ecuador. En route Sammy pointed out the beach on which he said he had found the gold and silver coins. We stopped to take a look.

It may have been a money beach but the only thing I could see were snakes, hundreds of them littering the sand. We watched as the gulls fed on the dying serpents, then died themselves for their appetites.

Many of the snakes were still alive and they did not seem to have any sense of direction. As the breakers washed them in, some wriggled back into the surf. Others would go in the wrong direction. Once out of the water — a snake would not go far. It would move perhaps twenty to thirty feet on land, then lay there seemingly exhausted waiting to die.

They had apparently been caught in the cold waters of the Humboldt Current that moves north from Antarctica, up the west coast of South America. The huge breakers had thrown them inshore.

Now that airline ticket back to the United States was really burning a hole in my pocket. Tory watched the snakes in fascination, but did not seem frightened by them. Sammy's concentration was deeper than ever. I don't think he even heard me when I asked, "What other kinds of cancer do you have here?"

The resort, which had been described to me as one of the best in all Ecuador, looked like a scene from an old Humphrey Bogart movie. It was posh late Depression. However, I have lived in worse places while treasure hunting. Not much, but worse.

One of the things that made the investors of World Wide believe Sammy had done all the footwork for the project was that he had said he arranged for a boat for us while we were there.

We went to see the man who was to loan us the boat. After several hours conversation, it became apparent he had no intention of even offering us a ride, much less letting us use it.

As we left, Sammy said, "I can't understand it. He must've changed his mind."

My only thought was, I wonder if I can get Sammy to join the gulls for lunch on the beach.

But we were there and we had to find a boat from which to work. In Florida that's not much of a problem; Ecuador was a different story.

The next morning we headed for the docks in Salinas and unhappily discovered no one was interested in renting a boat to us. By the end of the day there were only two we had not checked out. One belonged to an American who worked for one of the oil companies. He had a twenty-six-foot, twin-engine inboard that was old and not too seaworthy.

The engines clanked and sputtered and the fumes were sickening. Yet as bad as it obviously was, we wanted to rent it. After two hours of dickering over price, the boat was ours for a month for $800. That was more than the boat was worth, but we had no choice.

We named it *The Pig* and left Tory there to see if he could make some of the necessary repairs. I had to check out the mag to make sure it was functioning properly. That at least was perfect.

After charging the mag's batteries all night, we were ready to start. Before we were out of the harbor, *The Pig* blew a gasket and we had to pull back in. The next day the engines were still being worked on. Waiting around, Sammy's unfulfilled promise of a good boat from which to work while we were in Ecuador began to bug me. I was short tempered with him.

However, the next day we finally did get out of the harbor and headed for the offshore waters of the money beach. The water was rough, and when we tried to round the point at Santa Elena, *The Pig* was more underwater than above. Swells and whitecaps were peaking at about twelve feet. To continue would have been useless . . . fatal is probably a better word.

Tory turned *The Pig* around and we spent the day magging out of an area on the north side of Santa Elena. Nothing.

The following day the wind was still blowing so we continued to search the area north of Santa Elena. At about 2 p.m. we got a hit. Tory went over the side. When he surfaced, he said, "Can't see a thing. The visibility is less than five feet."

"Try again," Sammy said.

Tory agreed. "OK, but I think I'll have better luck if you lower an anchor line to just off the bottom. I'll ride it and you can pull me along until I spot something."

"Good idea," Sammy said. Sammy, by the way, had not yet donned his own wet suit. "But let's move from the deeper water toward the cliff," he told Tory.

"No way. That's dangerous."

"I'm in charge," Sammy blurted angrily. "You'll do as I say."

Tory grinned. I was beginning to like Tory very much. "I'll tell you what," Tory said to Sammy. "You drag on the anchor and I'll pull you."

For the next ten minutes the verbal exchange was hot and very salty. In the end Sammy agreed to do it Tory's way, which was the only sensible thing he could do. Tory reasoned if he was being towed from deep water towards the cliff, the water would get shallower and shallower. With only five feet of visibility he could easily be pulled into a coral head.

Whatever, it was apparent Sammy did not want to get into the water. That night, back at the hotel, Tory came to my room.

"Hey, Roy," he said, "can I move in with you?"

He had been sharing a room with Sammy.

"Sure," I said. "Glad to have you."

Tory and I quickly became good friends. The next day he confided that "If it wasn't for you, Roy, I'd pack up and head back to the States. That bastard really burned me yesterday. I don't think I'll forget it."

The Pig made it out of the harbor before one of the engines conked out. We returned to the dock.

"I've had it with this boat," I told Sammy. "There's no way that we can run any kind of an operation from this piece of junk."

We contacted the owner and received a refund for the unused portion of the month still remaining.

The day was spent unloading our equipment from *The Pig*. With that done we headed back to the resort. Once there we contacted the owner of a thirty-two-foot boat called the *Scuba*. We were there in the off season for tourists so the boat was rented to us for $250 a week instead of the normal $90 a day. We had it for a month.

Unlike *The Pig*, *Scuba* was a sound boat and new throughout. By late in the afternoon we had our equipment reloaded but there was nothing we could do for the day. A watchman was hired to keep an eye on our equipment.

"He looks like a snake," Tory remarked.

"Yeah," I agreed.

"Maybe we ought to hire a watchman to watch him."

Returning to the resort, we stopped the truck and walked down to the water's edge for another look at the sea snakes that were still being washed ashore.

Most of them were about three feet long. Their backs were solid black; their stomachs a bright orange. Tory picked one up with a stick. It turned its head trying to get away from the stick. Using the stick, he pried open its mouth. The fangs were small.

Now we knew the snakes were not aggressive, at least not on land. They would bite only when given no other alternative. The small fangs were a blessing. We figured if we wore a complete wet suit and thick gloves there was not much chance they would hit us and do much damage.

In our off hours, of which there were lots while we were trying to work with *The Pig*, I talked to many people about the coins on the beach. Unfortunately few spoke English, but those who did had heard the story about the coins.

One day I went metal detecting on our money beach. When I had a violently wriggling sea snake thrown at my feet, I moved to other pastures . . . one of the ancient burial mounds nearby. However, the detector was not functioning properly and all I received for my trouble was exercise.

I was beginning to learn about the people, who seemed to have a very casual attitude regarding sanitation, at least by the standards I had encountered elsewhere. Pigs and chickens were as welcome in the houses as were the children. Americans, however, were not. Generally the average person did not like Americans. It seems that every time a United States ship put in, the crew on liberty always got into trouble.

In my conversation with the local residents I began to think perhaps there was more than one shipwreck offshore. Sometimes the coins were described as being irregular, at others they were said to be round, which would indicated a much later period. But always gold and silver were washed ashore. We knew the Spanish thirty-four-gun frigate *Leocadia* was reported to have gone down here in a storm on November 7, 1800. However, most of its treasure was supposed to have been salvaged. **Most.**

During one off afternoon when the weather was so rough we did not even try to go out, I stood on a cliff and watched the rollers coming in, breaking ten to twenty feet high. In a storm what would it be like, I wondered? I could understand how a ship, maybe more than one, might have foundered in that boiling water. Certainly the wave action was such that coins could wash ashore.

We wished we could have seen some of the coins but the people there were too poor to hang onto them long. It made me a little sick inside when I learned most of the coins had been melted down and sold to the local bank just as gold and silver. History in a melting pot.

The first time out in the *Scuba* we were able to round the point and begin to mag our area. We had to stay out because the surf was too rough to work inshore. Using the fathometer we found several shallow areas just below the surface — reefs, one about eighteen feet beneath the surface.

It was here I had another hit. The magnetometer showed only a small area, but the gamma change was enough to make us want to take a look. Tory and I went over the side. If there was ferrous material, it might be a trailing to our wreck.

At the bottom of the reef, which was forty-five feet beneath the surface, we found a large ballast pile. At last we had something. As Tory and I started to surface, we realized we had plenty of company. Sharks would come out of the darkness and pass us, then turn around and pass us again. There were so many of them the thought of sea snakes never entered our minds. When we surfaced, we fairly lept into the boat.

The weather was getting worse and the water rougher. Tory didn't say anything, but I could see on his face that we had better try to make it around the point and back to the harbor before it was too late. Sammy looked sick and I could tell Tory had been struggling to fight off Montezuma's revenge. We headed back.

Tory Dowsett at the stern of the Scuba *in Ecuador.*

(Roy Volker Photo)

Now, at least, we knew we had a wreck. The question was its identity. Was it the *Leocadia* or one of a much earlier period, the 1700 wreck, the coins from which Sammy had induced World Wide to back this project?

The following day the sea was too dangerous for us to try to make it around the point. Being stuck onshore, I broke out my metal detector, which I had repaired, and called for Sammy to join me on the beach. Within an hour we found three dated pieces of eight — 1700, 1699 and 1697. All had the Lima mint mark and all showed water wear. By the end of the day we had found another four coins but I was ambivalent about Sammy. We seemed to have a wreck — by this time I was sure of it — yet Sammy was a little too introspective and uncommunicative to suit me.

Another day of bad weather and I was out on the beach alone. Tory had been struck down by the drinking water, but Sammy just didn't want to come along. He said he was sick but by then I was beginning to suspect anything and everything Sammy told me.

I worked the beach myself that morning and found another coin. Later in the day I decided to try for the ancient Indian burial mounds again. I detected for hours and did not get a single reading. But as soon as I put a shovel into one of the mounds, I uncovered pottery, hand-engraved beads, and several little figures of clay. One was a whistle shaped like a man. No gold.

For the next two days the wind kept blowing and I kept trying to induce Sammy to return to the beach with me. By now I, too, had recalled that great American slogan for people traveling overseas: "Don't drink the water!" It was too late, but I was not going to spend my time suffering in that crummy hotel. I wanted to spend it on that snake-covered beach. I was becoming braver about them.

"Hey, man, let's go out," I said to Sammy.

He refused, saying, "I'm not interested in finding a few coins. The effort isn't worth it. I'd rather go for the big one in the water."

Now that was not the Sammy I remembered, the Sammy who'd pick up junk off wrecks to sell as scrap. I knew him well enough by now to know if he thought he had a chance of finding one gold

An amphora found by Roy Volker in Ecuador in 1967.
(Dick Richmond Photo)

or silver coin, he would be out there hunting. I could see in his eyes the story he told us when he showed the World Wide people those two handfuls of coins might have been twisted a little to suit his purpose.

"Where did you get those coins you showed us in St. Louis?" I demanded.

"Off the beach."

"Bull!"

"I did."

"You're a lying little bastard and if you don't tell me the truth, I'm going to take a pair of pliers and pull your nose off."

Sammy stared at me in horror. "You wouldn't?"

"All I need from you is one more lying word."

Sammy looked out the window when he answered. "I found some of the coins," he said. "The others I bought off the locals. So what?" he said, belligerently. "It got you here, didn't it? You found coins yourself, didn't you?"

"Yeah," I agreed, my anger subsiding. I really believed a treasure wreck was buried off our money beach by now, but I still didn't like Sammy. I wanted to know from whom he had purchased the coins. When I found out, I hired a young man, who spoke English fluently, to act as my interpreter.

Some of the people came to the beach with my young interpreter

Volker with a clay pipe he took from a sunken wreck at Nassau. The ship had gone down 300 years ago. (Dick Richmond Photo)

and I asked them to show us exactly where they had found the coins. Each told us the story of the storm and the tidal wave.

In 1932 there was a hurricane. Almost immediately after it passed a small tidal wave struck the beach at Punta Canero. When the water subsided, people started finding coins. There were so many a representative from a bank in Guayaquil set up a table on the beach and purchased the coins for half their bullion weight. The coins were later melted down and resold for their weight in gold and silver.

I was determined to find that wreck offshore and through my interpreter asked when the sea calmed down. I was told we had arrived at the wrong time of the year. In January, February and March the water was calm and became much clearer.

In the telling of the story everything seems condensed. Sammy had called me in February, but it was November before we finally arrived in Ecuador. Things happened in bunches, but there was a lot of space between some of the bunches. Weeks of preparation had stretched into months. Now I could understand why Sammy became so quiet when we arrived. The ocean he had seen was flat and not like this. There were no shark hunts or sea snakes. He knew about the snakes, but when he had been here, he was not finding them on the beach. Knowing this, I liked Sammy even less. He had not done his homework very well. But now I understood him better.

As long as we were there, I was determined we were going to work that wreck. I knew I could find it. But if we were going to work it, we would need an airlift; and a compressor larger than the one presently aboard the *Scuba*.

Driving into Guayaquil, we took a room in the Majestic Hotel and then went about purchasing equipment needed for a five-inch airlift. We found a motor and a compressor large enough to do the job. Both were in disrepair and had to be fixed. Because they were broken, they were rented to us for three weeks for $125. It took most of the day to find the parts to make the repairs.

As Tory was making repairs and I wandered the city looking for parts, I saw a starving dog being chased by a cat. I fed the dog. Seeing a cat was unusual. People there, I was told, ate cats. If true, it might account for the reason we saw so many rats.

About midnight we heard gunshots. We learned nothing about the firing, but a week before our arrival there had been a student demonstration. The demonstration turned into a riot, and during the disturbance the students threw Molotov cocktails at soldiers and police. The police had opened fire cutting down several rioters.

Eventually we grew used to the rich, spicy food, but after hearing about the cats, I never asked what was in it. Tory and I began to mix with the locals and got on very well. Sammy stayed in his hotel room most of the time when he was not out with us on the boat. He found more and more reasons why he could not go into the water. He was becoming an irritant for other reasons as well.

When in Guayaquil, we heard a German by the name of Brunner was screaming about us being there. He was claiming he had the only treasure-hunting permit and he wanted us out of the country. This threw Sammy into a panic and for days we sat around because he did not want to go out until he was able to get a permit and protection.

In spite of Sammy, the first day the water calmed we took the *Scuba* out to search. The boiling surf kept us from getting as close to shore as we wanted, but we covered a large area in the offshore waters.

Late in the afternoon, Tory and I decided to make an exploratory dive in a shallow area where we had had a few hits on the mag. Swimming the length of the reef, which dropped from fourteen feet to forty-five feet rather quickly, we found some ballast stones and fire brick but nothing else. The wreck appeared to have hit the high part of the reef, then went down on the seaward side. That was the guess, but over the years I had learned anything could happen in a storm. Wrecks are seldom where they're supposed to be.

Regardless, I did not think this would be our treasure wreck. It was too far from shore — at least a half mile. Coins would not travel that far even in a tidal wave. Those on the wreck just below Fort Pierce had traveled further. However, the conditions were different, the water there is all shallow. Here it was fairly deep.

In spite of the fact I didn't think it was the wreck we were after, we decided to dig a few potholes with the airlift the next time out. There might be more there than met the eye.

What did meet the eye were large packs of ever-present sharks. In that murky water diving was spooky, but Tory was always there with me. If a shark got too nosey, he was there to push it away with a bang stick. Friendship between two men really grows under those conditions.

Sammy? Well, Sammy stayed aboard the *Scuba* thinking of reasons why he couldn't get into the water and why he wouldn't set a percentage for Tory then and there.

Tory wanted to know and since Sammy wouldn't tell him, I gave Tory an answer that satisfied him.

The days that followed were long and unproductive. There is nothing more boring than doing a magnetometer survey of an area clean of wrecks and debris. Even a little modern junk in the water helps to hold the interest. But one morning the water calmed to a point where it was almost flat.

I looked at Tory and grinned as we rounded the point and moved in toward our money beach.

"Today's the day, Tory," I laughed. "We're going to find the big one. We'll put the *Scuba* right up on the beach if we have to."

Heading the *Scuba* in, we worked a grid pattern, moving closer and closer to shore. When our fathometer showed we were in about thirty-five feet of water, we were about 150 feet off the beach.

It was late afternoon and we still had not hit a thing. Then we swung and made a pass a little closer.

"Hit," I yelled.

Sammy threw a buoy.

"Run her again."

"Hit," I yelled on the second pass.

Sammy threw another buoy. Same spot.

"It's a big one," I yelled, laughing. "Big!!!"

We were in thirty-one feet of water, less than 150 feet offshore. The wreck was lying parallel to the beach.

Suiting up, Tory and I went over the side and tried to find the wreckage, but the bottom was all white sand and nothing showed. The wreck was there and it was buried.

"Good," I thought. "A virgin."

Just as I was thinking "virgin," several sea snakes swam by, but they did not pay any attention to us. We did not mind being ignored in the least.

We did not know it then, but Sammy was about to stick it to us. That German was really worrying him so he went to see his friend, the one who didn't lend us his boat. The friend put him in contact with a lawyer. Sammy wanted a lease. His friend told him about the length of red tape in Ecuador, but that did not deter Sammy.

"Look!" his friend said to me, "you can work the site and I will make sure you are protected."

This was a business gesture I understood very well and was willing to let it go at that. The man was saying in effect that he was the top dog in those parts and with a percentage to him and to a few others we could work to our hearts' content. A lease would just foul things up.

But Sammy wanted the lease and we had to go to Guayaquil to meet with lawyers to see if we could obtain one. One hour with an overly cautious American lawyer is enough to drive a man up a wall. A day with a South American counterpart drives a man to insanity.

The following morning Tory and I loaded the airlift and compressor aboard the *Scuba* and took off for our site. We promised Sammy we would stay off the big wreck close to shore, but at least we'd be able to pot some holes near the reefs where we found the ballast and fire brick. While one of us worked, the other had to stand guard. The water was murky and the sharks were monsters.

While I was on the airlift, I tried not to look. I could feel Tory standing next to me. I felt as long as he was there, I was safe. It's kind of like shutting your eyes and hoping that no one sees you.

We found a length of cable. It indicated what we were digging on at the reef had to be a more modern wreck than the one for which we

Volker with I. R. Rolle Jr. at Fort Montegue in Nassau dig for coins on the beach. Volker is demonstrating the sensitivity of a new White's metal detector.
(Dick Richmond Photo)

were searching. It could have been the *Leocadia.*

At dinner that evening Sammy was pretty gloomy when he sat down with us.

"That Brunner is a pretty tough customer," he moaned.

"So."

"There are goons here who will do anything for a few bucks. Maybe we should leave now and come back later. When we get a lease, we'll have the law on our side."

"Up yours."

"Remember, Roy," Sammy said, "if this guy sees us digging out there, we'll be showing him where our wreck is, then what's to keep him off if he has a legal right?"

"We're not leaving," I said, "but you have a point about us not showing him where the wreck is. I'm willing to hold off digging for a week or two, but I'm not going home until we make a dig. I want to know if what we have is what we came after. If it's a dud, we're not coming back."

For the next two weeks we magged out in the bay. From the boat we could see several cars parked on the road with people in them watching us. Every time we got a reading we dove, but found nothing but a few pieces of modern junk.

Then one day the weather turned calm and Tory and I decided to dig on the first wreck we'd found, the one with the huge ballast pile. Sammy was with us. As usual, he stayed on deck.

Throughout the day, one man stood guard poking at sharks that came too close as the other man potted holes. Before we finally called it quits we had potted about thirty holes.

At one point we were working in water as deep as fifty-eight feet. All we found was one small piece of pottery and more brick and ballast. From that we guessed the rest of the wreck had to be in the breakers.

We surmised the ship was driven inshore by the storm and when she hit the reef, her bottom was torn out and she dropped her ballast. The top part of the ship may have hung up on the reef for a short time, but then it, too, was smashed and carried inshore. There she dumped whatever she had been carrying.

Because we were working so deep, we had to decompress and call it a day. In the afternoon the water again was flat. Sammy and I decided if it was that flat the next morning we were going to make a dig on whatever it was in thirty-one feet of water off our money beach.

The next day the ocean was calm and the road was free of spectators. Within an hour after we were aboard the *Scuba*, Tory and I anchored over the wreck and suited up. We had trouble setting the anchors and could not understand why. Eventually, however, we did get them set and Tory and I went over the side. As was now his custom, Sammy watched over the compressors for our hookahs and our airlift.

Considering the water was just starting to grow calm, it was fairly clear, which was good because within seconds after we were on the bottom Tory and I were circled by four large sharks.

Popping to the surface, we grabbed our bang sticks and dropped back to the bottom. As Tory dug, I watched. No damn sharks were going to keep us from finding out what we wanted to know. I was so angry I wanted one of them to come in close enough for me to blow off his head. But none of them did and within five minutes they swam away.

Sharks, Sammy, the lawyer, the German, or anything living was going to keep us from our wreck. What did it was coquina, a limestone of broken shells and sand cemented together like the hardest concrete.

We dug hole after hole and each time we got down to about three feet we ran into the coquina. We could not dig through it and there was no way of chipping through. By the time we reached the surface, tired and exhausted, we knew the only way we would crack it was with dynamite. For us, at that time, dynamite was out of the question.

Now we knew with what we were faced. But we were not prepared for what we found. Homework! A man always has to do his homework. The coins had been found after storms. How could we know the ship was locked beneath the coquina? The rental of the boat was up in two days and it had already been leased to someone else for the next thirty.

It was almost Christmas and Sammy and Tory wanted to be home with their families. I didn't want to leave without blowing a big hole in the center of that coquina, but there was little we could do in the time remaining.

In retrospect, I realize how that ship could be beneath the coquina and how the coins were thrown on shore. The tidal wave of 1932 had apparently cracked the crust and the great surge of water had lifted the coins out and thrown them about. Over the years the coquina had sealed the cracks, again burying the ship from view. How I wished I could see what was there.

I was willing to stay and see if I could find some way of dynamiting. Tory would have stayed with me, but pain was once again my enemy and I was being defeated by that agony in my back. I was eating pills to ease the suffering. My right foot was dragging because my leg was becoming numb.

There was no alternative. Two days after I arrived back in St. Louis I was in the hospital. Several disks in my back were badly damaged. I was operated on. Following surgery, the doctor told me that it would be a year before I would be free from pain.

Because it now became apparent to everyone I wouldn't be able to return to Ecuador, World Wide decided it would be foolhardy to send anyone else with Sammy. The project was abandoned . . . the treasure is still there.

I never saw Sammy again, but Tory and I have become fast friends. We have shared a number of adventures together.

18

TWO-MAN EXPEDITION

AS MY BACK WAS MENDING, it curbed my immediate restlessness. I was again in the record business as the promotion director for Commercial Music. At the same time I opened a museum of sunken treasure in Clarksville, Missouri, which I later sold, and started a business called Search Electronics.

The firm was established initially to deal in the locating and recovering of sunken barges, shipwrecks, oil rigs and so forth. Later it was expanded so the thrust of the operation changed character. I became a distributor for White's Electronics, the largest manufacturer of metal detectors in the world. Also, I formed a corporation with Ken White Jr., Dick Richmond and Ed Kastner called Golden Royal Enterprises, a sea-going firm operating out of Nassau, Bahamas, in association with I. R. Rolle Jr., president of Commonwealth Explorers, Ltd. So again I became a full-time treasure hunter.

Many years passed between the trip to Ecuador and the formation of Golden Royal. It was in that period I took up in earnest the quest for Orellana's galleon.

I knew by heart the reports of the men who had attempted to salvage the *Maravillas* in the years after her sinking. There was some recovery of the treasure and the words of what was found rang in my head. Subtracting that from the total manifest meant there were millions remaining to be uncovered.

Many of the reports were filled with words of men seeking favor with the Spanish monarch, of charges of one man leveled against another, of backbiting and name calling. But some of those reports discussed honest problems of pinpointing the wreck, of ballast piled on top of the treasure, of not having enough divers or the right equipment. These were things of which I was familiar and they weighed my interest.

Conch Key had been eliminated; Cay Sal Bank was illogical. Los Mimbres had to be Red Riding Rocks or Memory Rock.

Red Riding Rocks are almost at the end of a small chain of islands. The Biminis are at the extreme north, then Gun Cay, North and South Cat Cay and Sandy Cay. Sixteen miles to the south is Orange Cay. The area is incredibly desolate with submerged reefs and fast-rising shoals everywhere. The amount of sand in the area is manifested by a silicon operation at nearby Sandy Cay. To me it seemed the reasonable place considering the sailing time Orellana had from Havana.

As far as Memory Rock was concerned, physically it was perfect. There is nothing around the area of that jut of rock popping out of Little Bahama Bank on the edge of the deep water for miles. The shoals there are even more treacherous than those at Red Riding Rocks and there are great pockets of sand all across the bank. The one thing that dissuaded me from searching there first was the distance. It seemed too far for Orellana to have traveled in the span of time he had. That was bad judgment on my part. Later I would regret my decision to search the Red Riding Rocks shoals first because I am blessed with remarkable hindsight.

World Wide was now out of the picture. Anything that was to be done I had to accomplish on my own. It was like starting over again, only worse. I was older, had the experience and should have known better. Yet I felt a strange affinity for Orellana, as if he were calling me. If he was, I sure didn't hear him clearly. Then there was the hard fact that I had acquired a goal in life, one that had not existed for me before. There was really no way for me to stop searching.

Of all the men I know who have taken up this unusual quest, Mel Fisher epitomizes this need to search. After he had uncovered those millions on the Colored Beach wreck, what he had found was important, what he was going to find next was even more important.

The responsibility I had had with World Wide had made me a planner, an organized man. I felt a debt to those who had put their trust in me and while I was working with World Wide, I left no ballast stone unturned trying to make that faith mean something. Working became a pleasure, the treasure a dream, the danger a stimulus.

Now I was responsible only to myself and to my family, yet those other things had become part of me, a part that could not be discarded. I was highly trained, good at what I did, yet with no real desire to attempt to form another outfit backed by people willing to invest in adventure. I was determined to at least try it on my own. And this determination is what started the run for the *Maravillas*.

Trying to put an expedition together from St. Louis is no mean task. Yet I had friends in Florida and I felt I could at least form a modest effort. How modest that first one would be I really had no idea.

Tory Dowsett had purchased a twenty-eight-foot open boat designed to catch porpoises. It was about twelve feet wide, rode flat on the water and had a low back end. The gas-engine operated vessel could attain speeds of 60 miles an hour.

Since it was designed for a specific purpose, it had none of the basic accouterments such as bunks, cooking facilities, a head or even shelter. Only a canvas canopy would protect us from the rain and the sun.

The entire expedition was to consist of three persons: Tory, Harold Still and myself. At the last minute Tory got a diving job in Puerto Rico and had to bow out. So it turned out to be just Harold and me.

When Harold left Dave Meinell and me in Grand Cayman, he returned to Miami and went into the insurance business. After a time he left that and went into the fast-food franchise business. He had done so well in Florida the state was literally overloaded with the franchise he was offering so his company was transferring him to California.

We wanted to make this trip together because both of us felt it might be the last time we would see each other for a long while. And it was the *Maravillas* in particular for which we wanted to search.

The *Flying Porpoise*, which had a range of about 400 miles, was loaded with canned food, a Coleman stove, water and two styrofoam ice chests that we filled to the brim with ice, soft drinks and all the other things we thought we might consume in two weeks.

The expedition was in July. We left Miami in the morning and arrived at Red Riding Rocks before noon. Immediately we started our magging operation. We were faced with a multitude of uncertainties regarding this wreck. Not only had our research placed Los Mimbres in four different locations, the depth of the water in which the *Maravillas* sank was listed on various pieces of information and was infuriatingly indefinite. This meant we were able to narrow the depth down to from eighteen to eighty feet, which takes in a lot of ocean.

However, we were not going to take any chances. We knew divers had worked on the wreck for a short time before it was completely lost under the sand and coral. It almost certainly would not be in depths greater than eighty feet. A free diver, even an exceptional one, cannot do much at that depth with the primitive salvage and diving equipment then available.

We had a fathometer aboard the *Flying Porpoise* and I had brought along the magnetometer sensing head with wings so it would sink to the depth I wanted. If the fathometer read eighty feet, we would let out seventy feet of cable and the head would fly about ten feet off the bottom.

Magging has to rank as one of the most boring jobs in the world when you are not finding anything, and that is all Harold and I did for two weeks. In that time we found one modern anchor and one very old one. The rest of the time we spent getting sunburned, dehydrated and reminiscing. Harold was his old self, joking and excited about the search. The entire time we were out, he never once lost his good humor.

The island behind which we anchored each night was loaded with birds that never seemed to shut up. Most of the time I was too exhausted to let them disturb me, but one night I could not sleep. I was restless and I blamed those birds and their insistent chirping for keeping me awake.

Harold was sound asleep when I took the .38 from my knapsack and fired. Blam, blam, blam. Harold jumped to his feet.

"What's wrong?" he asked, startled.

"Those birds. They were keeping me awake."

The birds by then, of course were half in flight and half still on the island but all of them were complaining and not in unison about my target shooting. We could see them circling above us in the moonlit sky.

"For crying out loud, Volker," he screamed at me. "Look at them now, you dumb bastard."

"Yeah," I said, looking at them now.

I still could not sleep, but neither could Harold and at least I had someone to talk to.

After a week we were about out of everything. On top of that we were grimy, baked and tired. We headed for Bimini, checked into a hotel, turned on the air conditioning. Then we went out to a restaurant and stuffed ourselves. Afterwards, we got drunk, then went back to the hotel and turned the air conditioning up to full blast before dropping off to sleep. We darn near froze to death. It was great.

The next morning we climbed into the *Flying Porpoise* and tipped our hats to Bimini as we headed back for Red Riding Rocks. We were there another six days electronically searching every square inch of that area. We had set up grids on a chart; back and forth we moved over the gridded area until that part was covered. Once eliminated, we marked it off the chart and moved into the next grid.

At about 2 a.m. on the sixth night after Bimini, we were hit by a sudden storm. We were getting wet, but we were all right until the wind shifted and moved the *Flying Porpoise* around so the stern was to the island.

"The anchor's dragging," Harold yelled above the noise of the wind and the waves crashing against the rocks.

"I know. I can feel it."

"It's going to have to be set or we're going to wind up on those rocks."

It was so black we couldn't see the rocks. We could barely make out the white foam of the waves thundering as they ran into the island and shot skyward. We knew we were moving closer because the noise was deafening.

Harold and I broke out our diving gear and an underwater light. The sea at night is a terrifying place. Sharks eat all the time, but they maraud in darkness. A light would attract them and we knew it. Yet we had no choice.

Neither Harold nor I looked at each other as we flipped over the side and grabbed the anchor line to follow it down.

The threatening noise above was immediately replaced with silence. It was an ominous silence of uncertainty and fear. We were in an alien environment in which we obviously didn't belong. We felt as if there were thousands of eyes watching us, waiting for us to make the slightest miscalculation.

Our one tether to safety was our anchor line. If we strayed away from it, or if we didn't set the anchor in time we would be two men with nowhere to go in a place where only the fit, the fast and the clever survived.

Hand over hand we moved, keeping together, flashing the light around to see if we could spot any dark moving shadows. The murky water in which we both had worked was nothing compared to this. In murky water a person could see a few feet all around. Here we could only see where the light was shining.

At last we found the anchor and set it. When we were both sure, we sped up the line like two children running from the bogeyman. Once aboard we removed our tanks.

"Spooky," I said, removing the rest of my equipment.

"Yeah," Harold agreed. "Spooky."

The remainder of the night was rough and Harold became sick. He did not get any sympathy from me because on our first expedition together, the one we had made years before with Art Hartman, Bill Settlemoir and George Traber, the rest of us had become seasick and Harold walked around eating peanut butter sandwiches. Patiently, I had waited for the opportunity to repay him. At last he gave me the chance.

I really did not want the chili, but I couldn't resist opening a can and cooking it so Harold would reap the same benefits he had presented to us. I went too far. The aroma was overwhelming even in the wind. It almost got me. Harold was still sick at daybreak.

Seaward the water was rough. In spite of that, I started plotting our next grid.

"It's too rough out there," Harold said.

I looked. "You're right," I agreed. "You wanna mag inside?"

Harold regarded me in silence for a time, then said, "Volker, I think you'd mag in a hurricane. I want to go home."

I never saw Harold after that trip. He moved with his family to California. I talked with him by phone once and he told me the franchise was not doing as well on the West Coast as it had in Florida. The next time I called his phone had been disconnected. I wrote, but he never answered. The letters were never returned.

Originally Harold was from Pittsburgh and I attempted to locate him there. I once heard he had moved to Kentucky, another story had him in Miami. I ran all the stories down, but was never able to locate him. None of our mutual friends have heard from him either. I expect one day to hear him scream at me over the telephone, "What do you mean I'm a screamer?"

19
END OF ONE RAINBOW

THE REST OF THE RED RIDING ROCKS area was quickly eliminated on the next expedition, which was a little better equipped than the one in which Harold and I had taken part. From there I moved to Little Bahama Bank, the last of the Los Mimbres locations.

Los Mimbres north of West End, Grand Bahama Island, lies about twenty miles from the nearest point of land and stands like a solitary and uninviting beacon for passing ships.

I could see in my mind the ancient navigators looking for that landmark as they sailed toward Bermuda, trying to keep it in sight to mark their positions, yet standing off far enough to insure they did not become one of the hundreds of victims of the shoals. The shallow reefs would tear the bottom from their deep-drafted vessels if they grew careless.

Before the search began, I had plotted the bank on my chart, marking off grids. It would be accomplished systematically so when I finished with one area, I would know what was there. Ships found would be marked, but not worked unless they appeared to be Orellana's galleon. Since I knew what to expect in this case, I would waste as little time as possible on those wrecks that did not shout "treasure" after a preliminary dig.

We found wreck after wreck. The bank is littered with them. Some we could discount immediately, others had to be dug. Each dig took time and time for me now had become the most precious of commodities. I was trying to find something that had been lost and buried under sand, coral and water for more than 300 years . . . and I was attempting to do it on two-week vacation expeditions.

It always seemed we would no sooner start than our two weeks

133

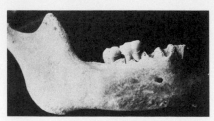

A human jaw bone found by Roy Volker on a wreck in the Bahamas in 1970.
(Dick Richmond Photo)

would be up. Yet little by little the bank was being methodically combed and marked off my grid pattern.

I had been at this for a while when in March, 1971, I was invited to put up a display at a coin show at the Gateway Hotel in St. Louis. It was something to do, but when the invitation came, it did not seem all that important. As it turned out, things were about to change for me again, and in a way I never thought possible.

In the booth next to me was Ed Moody, representing White's Electronics. It wasn't my introduction to metal detectors. However, from that meeting I was to turn into a hard-core enthusiast. With a metal detector I was to make the biggest single find of my life when I discovered the 1715 eight escudo Spanish Golden Royal, which has been valued at between $50,000 and $75,000. Eventually, I would co-author a book on the subject of metal detecting called "Treasure Under Your Feet."

I did not know it then, but as I was setting up my display, the co-author of that book, Dick Richmond, was about to walk in and chat with me. Dick would also share all my adventures in the years to come. Where I was a dreamer; he was pragmatic. He didn't know how to make my dreams come true, yet he figured ways in which to make them pay. In other words, he turned me around to a very practical way of thinking without giving up the rainbow chase.

What I remember about him then was that he carried himself easy as a man does who has no trouble fitting in anywhere. His conversation was casual and filled with the curiosity of a person who seems able to catalog things in his mind for ready reference. How well he did this, I would learn.

As we were chatting, he tried not to interfere with the things I had to do to get ready for the opening of the show, which was just a couple of hours away. Then a crew from one of the television stations came in and Dick handed me his card and said, "Call me when you're not so pressed. I'd like to talk with you again and perhaps do a feature story about you for the Post-Dispatch."

Dick is a feature writer and a columnist for the Post-Dispatch. It was two days before I had a chance to telephone. When I did, Dick invited me to the newspaper and we sat and chatted for several hours.

I invited him to visit my museum in Clarksville, Missouri, which is a two-hour drive from St. Louis. He took me up on the offer and brought with him Renyold Ferguson, one of the the photographers at the paper.

A semi-modern wreck found in 1970 by Roy Volker near Bimini in the Bahamas. *(Roy Volker Photo)*

It was a fast friendship and one of the closest I have ever enjoyed. During one of our conversations, I asked Dick to join an expedition I had planned for July.

"I'm not a diver," he responded.

"You can learn."

"OK," Dick said, grinning. "I'll go."

By this time I had the bank pretty well plotted and most of it covered. There wasn't too much left to search and I calculated with a reasonable amount of luck we would find the *Maravillas* on this trip.

As on a couple of voyages in the past, I had worked out an agreement with Art Hartman, who was by then the owner and captain of his own treasure-hunting boat, the 80-foot *Arto*. For expenses and a percentage of anything we found, Art would take us to search the area. It was the *Arto* that the members of Golden Royal Enterprises purchased years later. We renamed her the *Golden Royal.*

This particular crew was probably one of the most interesting and diverse of all those I had ever assembled. Besides Dick and myself were Ken White Jr. of White's Electronics, Don Paule and Ed Kastner of the St. Louis Underwater Recovery Team, and David Hoy, author-lecturer and an authority on extrasensory perception. Hoy was Dick's friend, and when Dick suggested I invite him along, I figured I had tried every other way to locate the *Maravillas;* having a famous psychic along couldn't hurt.

Roy Volker (left) and Dick Richmond.   *(Robert C. Holt Photo)*

Things were happening with Art of which I wasn't aware until a week or so before we were ready to go. On the first of May he had gone into partnership with Doubloon Salvage and for the next several seasons would head the best-equipped treasure-hunting outfit in the United States to work the 1715 treasure fleet wrecks around Fort Pierce. In the middle of May he would find a sealed box off the *San Antonio,* one of the ships that sank in the 1733 disaster.

So as his mate for this trip was Sam Staples of Doubloon Salvage. There was to be another member of the crew as well. This one I did not learn about until we arrived in Miami to make the crossing to Bimini and then West End. The third member of Art's crew was Bob Marx, a treasure hunter and underwater archeologist who had spent almost three years uncovering the sunken pirate city of Port Royal, Jamaica.

From Dick's point of view as a writer the fact Marx was along was a fortunate accident. I didn't see it that way. To me he was just another treasure hunter, one I didn't know except by reputation and with whom I had no agreement — gentleman's or otherwise.

Marx was reading proofs of his now famous book, "Shipwrecks of the Western Hemisphere," but a sea voyage to perform this tedious work is not what he had in mind. As the marine archeology editor for Argosy magazine, he was doing a follow-up story on a "wall" that supposedly had been found at Bimini.

Buildings reportedly had been discovered beneath the water's surface at Andros Island and there was renewed talk of Atlantis

Dick Richmond, one flipper on and one flipper off, swims over a wreck site in the Bahamas on the expedition in search of Nuestra Senora de la Maravillas in 1971. Richmond had injured his foot in a fall.

(Roy Volker Photo)

being uncovered, spiced by one of the predictions of the so-called sleeping prophet, Edgar Cayce, who supposedly foretold that the continent would rise at Bimini in 1969. Since we were going that way Marx had prevailed upon his friend, Art Hartman, for a lift. He was paying for his fare by acting as a mate. In return Art promised him a day on the site.

When we arrived at Bimini, there was a large salvage vessel called the *Venture* over the "wall." The expedition included Dimitri Rebikoff, a French engineer and a pioneer in underwater exploration, underwater photography and underwater equipment such as the Pegasus, a kind of motorized sled for scuba divers.

Marx and Rebikoff were friends but a person would have never guessed it by their reactions to each other when they came face to face on the *Arto*. There was a lot of screaming and name calling, which was brought to an abrupt halt when Art stepped in.

I was confused by the whole thing, but between what Marx related and what I was able to piece together later, the story had others involved as well, including Dr. J. Manson Valentine, a naturalist and the honorary curator of the Science Museum in Miami, a group of Edgar Cayce followers, a pilot by the name of Robert Brush, and a large American corporation.

In 1967 Rebikoff, flying over an area at Andros Island, southeast

Art Hartman (foreground) who headed the magnetometer team on an expedition to Serrana Bank in 1974.

(Photo supplied by Art Hartman)

of Bimini, spotted from the air a rectangular object, which he estimated to be about a quarter of a mile long. But when he returned with Valentine, he could not find it.

Then in 1968, Brush, who was flying a cargo run for Southern Airways between Miami and Nassau, spotted some other rectangular shapes off Andros. This was at about the same time that Valentine found some pillow-shaped stones that looked to be a causeway or the top of a wall at Bimini.

Valentine was contacted by Brush and he and Rebikoff were taken to the site that Brush had spotted from the air. Some of the "structures" were only three feet beneath the surface of the water.

Marx said he had been at the site and filled me and the others in on what had been found and why he was with us.

"They found one rectangle," Marx related, "that measured 100 by 60 feet. I was there later. There are partitions on the east and southwest ends. Its floor plan is exactly like the one of the Temple of the Turtles at Uxmal in the Yucatan."

Dick raised his eyebrows at that statement. Uxmal is about a thousand miles from Andros. Dick didn't say anything, but Marx is preceptive and noticed the questioning expression on his face.

"Why not?" he challenged. "What the hell, the Mayas had boats.

"About a mile from the rectangular shape that the pilot spotted," Marx continued, "Rebikoff and Valentine found two other buildings.

In the Florida archives building in Tallahassee during the opening of the box found by Art Hartman on a wreck near Marathon, Florida. From left (foreground): Carl Clausen, Florida state marine archeologist; Art McKee, treasure hunter; Art Hartman, treasure hunter; and Dollie Cole, wife of Edward N. Cole, president of General Motors. (Dick Richmond Photo)

Twelve other buildings have been found by other divers, including me.''

Marx said that it did not take long for the press to get wind of what was going on and investigating teams swarmed over the area like flies. Then the scholars took over, some of whom apparently did not bother to dive on the formations before offering their opinions. Followers of Edgar Cayce jumped on it, sure that Cayce had been correct once again. Others became involved. Then a rumor spread that two Americans had found two statues among the formations and had illegally spirited them back to the United States. The Bahamian government, which was not sure what was occurring on its biggest and most remote and largely uninhabited island of Andros, became disconcerted and called a halt to any further investigations.

From the sound of it, at least to Dick, the whole affair was marvel-

A view of the salvage vessel, the Venture, *anchored over the* "wall of Atlantis" at Bimini.   *(Dick Richmond Photo)*

ously ridiculous and really neat except for those who were seriously involved, which included Valentine and Rebikoff.

Marx went on to say that before the Bahamian government stopped the investigations, marble columns or pillars were supposed to have been discovered, as well as cut stone disks on a nearby cay in something that resembled an ancient ceremonial court.

To me it all sounded very suspicious. To Dick it was obviously exciting.

"Atlantis is always being 'found' by someone or another," Dick said. "Makes no difference to me. But if we're going to be diving on something man-made, it was just possible it's from an ancient civilization.

"Assuming that the land mass did not sink, but that the water rose since the time it was built, that would make those buildings and whatever we're diving on more than 10,000 years old. That would have to be during the Pleistocene, or Ice Age, when the sea was lower. Wouldn't that be a kick?"

I didn't know what Dick was talking about, but Marx seemed to. He nodded in agreement.

In 1969, Marx said he had convinced Argosy to sponsor an expedition to Bimini. Rebikoff was with him. This was the time of the reported "stolen statues" and after two days of diving, they were told by officials on Bimini to pull off. To continue they had to have permission from Nassau.

"We had some promised financial aid from an archeological society," Marx told us. "So we applied to the Bahamian government for excavation permits.

"Then last winter I read that a large American corporation had been granted exclusive rights on all the ruins around here."

"Why?" Dick asked.

"The corporation has a lot of land holdings on Bimini."

"I mean why would they want to?" Dick wanted to know.

Marx shrugged. "All I know is that when Rebikoff went to Nassau, he was told he couldn't explore the sites at Andros either."

Quite frankly I did not share Dick's fascination with the subject. I was interested in things man-made, too, but it had nothing to do with

Evidence of a wreck never found on the expedition in the Bahamas in 1971.
(Dick Richmond Photo)

walls or buildings out in the boondocks somewhere. If we were going to examine this thing, I wanted to do it and get on with the project at hand. The conversation, however, was not yet over.

"I can see that the corporation is apparently exploring," Dick said, "if the *Venture* is its ship."

"A geologist was hired," Marx said, "and then apparently it was decided to launch a full-scale expedition. There were a bunch of people asked to participate, including a number of psychics from the Edgar Cayce Foundation. Until about three days before the expedition was to start, I was supposed to be a part of it."

"What happened?" Dick asked.

Marx shrugged and slipped over the side into the water.

"Good," I thought, "at least, they can't jabber under water."

I would have jumped in immediately to take a look, but this was to be Dick's first dive in the ocean and I wanted to watch him. I needn't have worried. He was as at home in the water as if he had been doing it all his life. Why is it only me who had trouble getting started?

Several of us entered the water to look at this controversial site, which from the surface resembles a roadway of great pillow-shaped stones fitted together. Taking a deep breath, I dove the twenty-five feet to the bottom. Again I dove just to make sure.

Art and I popped to the surface at the same time. "My God!" I exclaimed. "Is that what all the fuss is about?! I've seen formations

Pillow-like formations that when discovered off Bimini were thought to be the "wall of Atlantis."   (Dick Richmond Photo)

like this lots of times. That's no wall."

Art grinned and headed back to the *Arto*.

An excavation had been started next to the "wall" so Dick and Don Paule put on tanks so they could inspect what had been done and to take underwater pictures. When Dick returned to the *Arto*, he shrugged and said, "It looks man-made, but it's probably a natural formation. Those stones are just lying on the bottom. One thing for certain; it's no wall."

Marx agreed with us when he returned, saying he had seen similar formations in the Yucatan. As far as I was concerned, that should have ended it. But no, we had to go searching for the "pillars," which to me resembled barrels of concrete without the barrels. We were wasting time and I resented it.

At last, however, I was given the opportunity to test my magnetometer. Ten minutes after the sensing head was let out, we had a hit. I was delighted because it was functioning perfectly.

Over the side we went. We found a wreck all right, the remnants of an American Civil War gunrunner. The South was supplied in part out of the Bahamas during that conflict. What we were seeing was one of the victims of the shoals.

The ballast pile was of great irregular-shaped rocks. Anchors and cables were all over the place, and there were more fish than I had ever seen in one place before. The wreck, which is in thirty feet of water, had become a reef.

This was the Arto *after it was purchased by Volker and company and renamed the* Golden Royal. *At the stern are the propwash blowers.*

(Dick Richmond Photo)

To me it was just so much trash. However, for Dick and some of the others it was their first wreck and they could not get enough of it. Borrowing my underwater camera, Dick put on a tank and dove to take some close-up pictures.

He was alone down there and I snorkeled over the wreck to watch. Where there are lots of little fish, there are usually big fish, and I had promised Dick's wife, Charlotte, that I would look out for him.

Sure enough a great barracuda, curious beasts that they are, swam up next to him. Barracudas with their baleful eyes and tooth-filled slump jaws that are always working as if they are chewing are menacing-looking animals.

Dick saw it. He turned, raised the camera and took its picture. Then he went swimming off with the barracuda right alongside him to photograph something else.

Back on board the *Arto,* I said to Dick, "Who was your friend?"

He grinned. "Are all barracuda that big? That damn fish stayed with me the entire time I was down there."

"He was sizing you up for a meal."

"Naw," he said, laughing. "**She** was romantic."

Hauling anchor, we headed for West End, Grand Bahama Island. En route, we found another rubbish wreck. I was starting to glow. It's that feeling a person gets at poker when he thinks he has an unbeatable hand. Orellana's galleon was nearby; I could sense it.

As the days passed, we found wreck after wreck. We were closing

Yellowtails swarm around the large ballast of a gunrunner that sank off Bimini during the American Civil War.

(Dick Richmond Photo)

in; the search area was growing smaller and smaller. If we just had enough time, I knew we would find it; I could almost feel Orellana calling out to me.

Then I began having trouble with my magnetometer. There was water in the cable, and by the time I realized what was wrong we lost a day and a half. In the meantime we resorted to dragging divers behind the boat to see if we could spot something that would give us a clue, something that would lead us to the *Maravillas.*

There were plenty of willing dragees, including Dick and David Hoy, but all anyone was finding was fish and coral. In dragging behind a boat the size of the *Arto,* the strain on the arms and legs is intense. After thirty minutes a person is exhausted, after forty-five you feel as if you might come apart at the joints.

After somewhere between thirty minutes and forty-five, Dick and David climbed aboard and slumped down on the deck to be replaced by two others. I was sitting next to them working on the mag.

"Why do they do that?" David asked Dick.

"I don't know, but it sure makes me nervous."

"There are so many of them, too."

"Yeah. I felt like bait."

That conversation may sound cryptic to you, but I understood every word. They were talking about the way barracuda will spot a person when he is being dragged, then come right up at him and trail in his wake. It is a very disconcerting experience.

Dick and David were no sooner aboard than I spotted a conch boat and directed Art to head for it. As we closed in, the air pollution became terrible and I saw Dick and David look at each other.

Roy Volker (left) and Dick Richmond board the Arto *in 1971.*
(Art Hartman Photo)

"Richard!" David said in a tone of admonishment.

"It isn't me, man," Dick protested.

Both eyed me as if I were a dead fish rotting in the sun.

"It isn't me either," I said, and pointed to the concher, which was still a hundred yards off.

The conch is an animal that lives in a beautiful shell, beautiful, that is, once it has been cleaned and deodorized. The animal can be eaten raw. When it is, it has the taste and consistency of boiled lobster that has been chilled.

Bahamians use it mostly in soups and stews. To prepare it, one first has to remove it from the shell, beat the hell out of it, marinate it for a couple of days and then boil it until tender.

I like it, but Dick's opinion in considerably different. "That," he said, "is a lot of trouble for something that has the consistency of foam rubber and the flavor of spoiled carp."

At the time of the voyage, Marx had recently spent several months in the Bahamas searching for wrecks, probably Orellana's galleon. Since I had not yet figured out what was wrong with the mag, I thought perhaps the fishermen might give us a clue. Marx told me he remembered seeing cannons lying on the edge of the deep water somewhere near Memory Rock. I should have known better, but I felt it was worth a look. At the time we were not finding a thing.

Fishermen who had spent their lives looking into the sea might know where they were. The captain did, and ten minutes later we

Marine archeologist Robert F. Marx and a Bahamian fisherman, in 1971, stand on the bow of the diving boat Arto *looking for signs of a ship that sank at the edge of the deep water north of West End, Grand Bahama Island.*   *(Dick Richmond Photo)*

were over an area in which there were cannons scattered all over the place in ten feet of water.

The cannons were British. The *Maravillas* would not have been carrying British cannons, at least not all British cannons, and Marx knew it. On top of that it wasn't even a wreck. The cannons had been dumped.

That night we moved into West End for a little shore time. As the others visited the mammoth Jack Tar Hotel I went over my chart. Dick, who had injured his foot and was not yet up to walking, stayed with me.

"Looks like you've almost covered the area," Dick said.

"Almost."

"Time is running out."

I nodded. "If we don't find it tomorrow, we'll have to hang it up for this trip. At least the mag is OK. I found the trouble. It was in the cable."

We were at the far end of the dock, away from most of the other boats. It was early night and many of the boats had their lights on. The lights glimmered on the water in a scene that was beautiful but was no competition for the orange moon that seemed to be rising out of the center of the island.

Dick stood quietly watching the spectacle. "We need our own

Ken White Jr. tests an underwater detector on a wreck site in the Bahamas.
(Dick Richmond Photo)

boat,'' he said. ''There has to be a sensible way for a man to do this. We can make it pay if we can get organized. We don't have to find big treasures to make it profitable. One thing I do know is that hitchhiking like we're doing here on Hartman's boat is not the answer.''

There was nothing particularly profound in what he was saying; it was the way in which he was expressing himself. The wheels were turning and I sensed he was trying to figure out how we might be able to keep that orange moon.

''We'll buy our own boat when we find the *Maravillas,*'' I said. ''I'll be ready tomorrow.''

And I was, but Orellana's galleon was not to be mine. In September, 1972, fourteen months later, Marx found the remains of the main part of the ship in thirty-seven feet of water in the one area I had not searched.

In truth, now that the emotion has passed, I guess I sensed I would lose the discovery to Marx from the moment he stepped aboard the *Arto*. Marx had all the research I had and more. He was an experienced treasure finder. More importantly, he had told Dick he soon would be backed financially. There was nothing to stop him. The race was on, and I was going to be left at the gate.

The reports began coming in that lots of silver was being taken from the wreck. Gold, however, was never mentioned. I began to wonder if the entire ship had been discovered. The gold would have been kept in the sterncastle beneath the captain's quarters. The

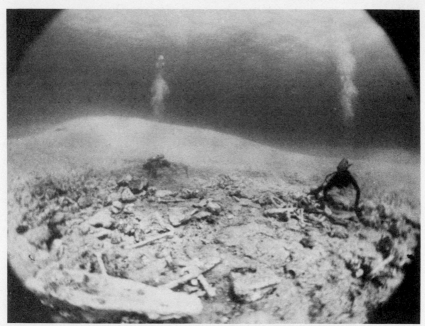

Photo taken with fish-eye lens shows divers swimming over the rubble that marks the grave of Nuestra Senora de la Maravillas, *which sank on Little Bahama Bank in 1656. This picture was taken by Art Hartman in 1974.*

silver could have been stored in the hold. If that were the case, then the most valuable part of the *Maravillas* treasure could still be missing.

Then in September, 1975, Dick and I were with Ken White Jr. aboard White's 57-foot vessel, the *Tamiron,* at the conclusion of an expedition after another treasure when a telephone call came in from Freeport, the Bahamas. By this time Marx was no longer taking part in the salvage of Orellana's galleon. The phone call was from the man in charge of the treasure recovery group.

Ken has developed some sophisticated underwater metal detectors through his firm, White's Electronics, and what the caller wanted was his help in locating the unfound treasure.

At that moment I knew for certain what previously I had only suspected. The *Maravillas* had broken apart in that terrible storm of January, 1656. The most valuable part of the treasure has still not been found. A picture of what might have happened began to formulate in my mind.

§   §   §

No one aboard the Maravillas *could see the huge wave that capsized the ship. The eyes held nothing but that terror-filled blackness of not knowing. It was the surge upward that Orellana felt as the wave picked up his galleon, then dropped her on the bank with such crushing force it broke her back.*

The main part of the ship, which held the bulk of the silver, sank immediately. Some of the crew clung to life on sections of broken planking. Most were swallowed by the sea, sucked below by the sudden plunging of the large vessel to the bottom.

Orellana was on the sterncastle when the galleon broke apart. The violence of the sea had thrown him against the cabin knocking him unconscious. When he retained his senses, a surge of hope rushed through his entire being; the sterncastle was still afloat. It was being pushed deeper onto Little Bahama Bank.

He was alone yet he smiled at being alive. The gold and the jewels were still all right; he would make it to safety and be a rich man. A vision of his wife went through his mind. She was so beautiful, but she was unaffectionate. His fame and fortune would make her want to cover him with kisses, love him until he had to seek refuge somewhere. The Spaniard smiled at the thought because he knew he would let her find him again to love him more.

Orellana raised his face to the unseen heavens in thanks just before he realized the sterncastle was sinking, too. It was going down a distance from the main part of the ship.

The panic the captain had felt earlier did not trouble him this time. He knew now he would die there with his ship. With that as a certainty a strange thought entered his mind: "How far would my grave be from the others?"

§   §   §

How far . . . and in which direction?

Somewhere near this solitary cay called Memory Rock is Orellana's gold.

(*Dick Richmond Photo*)

You have just finished reading a marvelous adventure story made wonderful because it is all true. If you enjoyed it, may we suggest you share your experience and recommend IN THE WAKE OF THE GOLDEN GALLEONS to a friend.

OroQuest Press
Suite 003
Lewis & Clark Tower
9953 Lewis & Clark Boulevard
St. Louis, Missouri
63136

THANK YOU NOTE

To the several persons who came to our aid as we were preparing this book we are most grateful. Alphabetically: William C. Fogarty Jr., Gregory M. Franzwa, Robert C. Holt Jr., Ed Kohorst, Carol Mainini, Art Phillips, Charlotte Richmond, Jack Shaheen, Elaine Viets and Marge Volker. We hope we haven't forgotten anyone.